T0334574

Cambridge Elements ≡

Elements in Research Methods for Developmental Science
edited by
Brett Laursen
Florida Atlantic University

CHILDREN'S VOICES AND AGENCY

Ways of Listening in Early Childhood Quantitative, Qualitative and Mixed Methods Research

Jane Spiteri
University of Malta

CAMBRIDGE
UNIVERSITY PRESS

Shaftesbury Road, Cambridge CB2 8EA, United Kingdom

One Liberty Plaza, 20th Floor, New York, NY 10006, USA

477 Williamstown Road, Port Melbourne, VIC 3207, Australia

314–321, 3rd Floor, Plot 3, Splendor Forum, Jasola District Centre,
New Delhi – 110025, India

103 Penang Road, #05–06/07, Visioncrest Commercial, Singapore 238467

Cambridge University Press is part of Cambridge University Press & Assessment,
a department of the University of Cambridge.

We share the University's mission to contribute to society through the pursuit of
education, learning and research at the highest international levels of excellence.

www.cambridge.org
Information on this title: www.cambridge.org/9781009500470

DOI: 10.1017/9781009285407

First published 2024

A catalogue record for this publication is available from the British Library.

ISBN 978-1-009-50047-0 Hardback
ISBN 978-1-009-28539-1 Paperback
ISSN 2632-9964 (online)
ISSN 2632-9956 (print)

Children's Voices and Agency

Ways of Listening in Early Childhood Quantitative, Qualitative and Mixed Methods Research

Elements in Research Methods for Developmental Science

DOI: 10.1017/9781009285407
First published online: July 2024

Jane Spiteri
University of Malta

Author for correspondence: Jane Spiteri, jane.spiteri@um.edu.mt

Abstract: The increased international legislation emphasising children's participation agenda heightened the need for high-quality research in early childhood. Listening to young children asserts their participation, agency and voices in research, an approach commonly associated with qualitative research methods. This Element provides a novel perspective to listening to children's voices by focusing on research methods in early childhood studies that are broadly categorised as quantitative, qualitative, and mixed methods. Locating these research methods from a children's rights perspective, this Element is based on values that young children have the right to be involved in research irrespective of culture and context. Each section discusses how the different methodologies and approaches used in early childhood research align with the principles of children's participation and agency, as well as their right to express their views on matters that affect them. The Element concludes with a roadmap for future early childhood research and its ethical dissemination.

Keywords: children's voices, early childhood research, quantitative methods, qualitative methods, mixed methods

ISBNs: 9781009500470 (HB), 9781009285391 (PB), 9781009285407 (OC)
ISSNs: 2632-9964 (online), 2632-9956 (print)

Contents

1 Introduction and Overview

Historically, young children have been viewed as a vulnerable and dependent group, always in need of care and protection. Consequently, their ideas in research have not been captured to the same extent as adults or older children. Given the increased international legislation emphasising children's participation agenda, in recent years, there has been a move towards high-quality studies in early childhood education recognising children's ideas in research. A wider recognition of children's rights and their role as active social agents in their own lives has increased researchers' interest in listening to children's perspectives in matters affecting them (Sun et al., 2023). Such recognition has led to the development of a plethora of collaborative research methods that acknowledge children's right to meaningful participation in research areas that affect them.

This Element aims to support researchers, practitioners, and policymakers in eliciting the voices of young children (up to age eight) in research. It explores the approaches that early childhood researchers take at every stage of the research process – from the beginning, when formulating hypotheses and research questions, to choosing data collection methods, identifying research participants, analysing and interpreting data, and finally, to the dissemination of the findings to the broader public. More importantly, throughout this Element, the readers will be guided to conduct successful and ethical research with young children.

Research approaches in early childhood studies that recognise and value children's rights to a voice are broadly categorised as quantitative, qualitative, and mixed methods, with each method having its own merit. The choice of methodology depends on the research questions asked. Large-scale quantitative studies test theories and hypotheses using a deductive approach; qualitative studies provide unique insights into the realities of young children's lives that go beyond surveys, experiments, and hypotheses; whereas mixed methods research combines qualitative and quantitative methodologies in a single study. With these points in mind, this Element discusses how different methodologies can be applied in research with young children in order to afford them agency and voices in research, the key elements required for meaningful participation. Each section will discuss how diverse methods reflect children's agency and their right to a voice in matters that concern them.

1.1 Overview of Subsequent Sections

This Element has three main objectives. First, it locates early childhood research from a children's rights perspective, recognising children as active agents and experts in their own lives. A universally accepted definition of listening to children's voices does not exist. As a result, children's voices may be ignored or partially addressed. Here, voices refer to children's hopes, fears, intentions, and expectations; whereas agency implies the way children express their voices. Ultimately, children's agency and voices are interconnected. Second, this Element provides an understanding of why and how children's voices can be elicited in research using a variety of qualitative and quantitative methods, as well as mixed methods, involving young children as co-researchers. Third, this Element addresses ethical considerations that might emerge during the research process.

Consequently, the diverse paradigms and philosophical stances commonly adopted in early childhood education and research are explored. To that end, the major methods of conducting early childhood research are presented. Together, these methods encapsulate the powerful notion of children's agency that has direct importance to children's lives. They respect children's participation in research by giving them the right to express their views and opinions on all matters that affect their lives. The aim is to capture the richness of children's ideas and experiences while engaging with them, to enable them to communicate their lived experiences using an approach to data collection, analysis, and dissemination that gives researchers the opportunity to access knowledge and experiences as presented by children. All of this can be achieved while still conducting rigorous research that generates new understanding and allows researchers to encounter the nuances that are part of the children's daily lives. To make this Element more relevant, its contents draw on various examples of early childhood literature to help the readers understand the logic and mode of inquiry in early childhood research, thus highlighting interesting work conducted in the field. The promises, challenges, and pitfalls of early childhood research are explored to support the readers to critically decide for themselves which methodological paradigm to follow.

In brief, this Element renews the debate around high-quality research (quantitative, qualitative, and mixed methods) with young children and makes the case that these research methodologies offer special ways of generating new knowledge that is essential going forward. Not only that, but it also illustrates the challenges associated with the research methods used so that researchers can make informed decisions about their choice of methods when conducting research.

Finally, throughout this Element, and particularly in this last section, future directions are offered, reflecting the central argument of this Element, which places children's voices at the centre of policy, curricula, and pedagogy in the early years. This Element will be of benefit to early childhood researchers, practitioners, and policymakers, and will be a good resource for courses concerning research in the field.

2 Early Childhood, Education, and Research

This section discusses early childhood, the period from birth up to age eight, and how our understanding of children and childhood changed over time. It also briefly discusses the importance of early childhood education, the education of children from birth up to age eight (UNESCO, 2023), and its potential for human development and lifelong learning, and for research.

2.1 What Is Early Childhood Education?

Internationally, early childhood is recognised for its potential to lay the foundations for human development (UNESCO, 2023; UNICEF, 2019). Early childhood is thought to be the most significant period of human development that sets the foundation for cognitive, social, and emotional development that lasts a lifetime (OECD, 2018; UNICEF, 2019). From a pedagogical standpoint, a child's ability to learn during the early years is central to their development, learning, and well-being (OECD, 2018, 2022a). Over the years, international concerns for early learning helped pave the way for the United Nations to recognise for the first time the transformative potential of early childhood education, especially for the most vulnerable and disadvantaged children (United Nations, 2015). The unequivocal message here is that education, as a fundamental human right, is of utmost importance for human development (UNESCO, 2017, 2020). Influenced by the policies of supranational organisations, such as those proposed by the OECD, United Nations, UNESCO, and the World Bank, early childhood education has thus become a global phenomenon and a site where social expectations of child development that meet the social and political needs of a country, are established. The international focus on early childhood education aligns with its role in supporting early learning and for laying the foundations for children's success and achievements throughout a lifetime.

Practices in early childhood education have been largely influenced by the historical, social, and cultural norms that helped shape the dominant political, philosophical, and ideological stances and paradigms of thought. Consequently, our beliefs about what early childhood education and early childhood research are have changed over time and will continue to evolve. Over the past two decades, young children's participation in early childhood education programmes has significantly increased worldwide (OECD, 2022b). Yet access to early childhood education is largely influenced by the socio-economic orientations of countries. In the global North (rich and high-income), early childhood education is recognised as a 'public good', aimed at promoting social change and social mobility (Flewitt & Ang, 2020, p. 12). Therefore, children living in economically wealthy countries in the global North have wider access to, and are more likely to participate in, early childhood education than children living in economically poorer countries in the global South (low-to middle-income).

Starting in early childhood, good-quality education is important for children's development and future employment prospects (European Commission, 2021; OECD, 2018). Even though quality in early childhood education is a contested term, the aim of good-quality education is to improve children's well-being and development (Edwards, 2021; Fleer & van Oers, 2018; Slot, 2018). The benefits of good-quality early childhood education depend on two observational instruments that allow for international comparison between early childhood provisions worldwide – the measurable structural characteristics (staff-to-child ratio, group size, staff training, minimum space requirements and resources) and the process quality (social, emotional, physical interactions, and instructional quality) (Edwards, 2021; OECD, 2018, 2022a; Slot, 2018).

The international focus on early childhood education led to the emergence of a wide range of national and international research *with* and *about* children, learning, and education, significantly increasing our understanding of the multifaceted nature of contemporary early childhood experiences, highlighting the long-term benefits of good-quality early childhood education for children's cognitive development and well-being, especially for those from disadvantaged background (Flewitt & Ang, 2020). Yet existing empirical research indicates an ongoing need for robust empirical early childhood research that challenges us to rethink our understanding of children and childhood, and the paradigm shifts that occurred over time in early childhood research. This compels us to take a historical look at the contextualisation of 'the child', 'children', and 'childhood'.

2.2 The Child, Children, and Childhood

Childhood is a social construct that focuses on positioning children within a social context, often in relation to adults (James & Prout, 2015). The dominant narratives that concern childhood focus on the biological, physiological, and chronological factors that constrain and shape children's lives. Consequently, conceptualisations of the child, children, and childhood draw from different scientific disciplines, including sociology, developmental psychology, behavioural biology, neuroscience, and early childhood education to create theoretical and empirical research approaches. Our understanding of the child, children, and childhood is the result of a process defined by social and cultural beliefs, practices, and experiences, making notions of the child and childhood socially and culturally constructed within a particular context.

2.2.1 The Child

Internationally and legally, it is widely accepted that a child is a person under the age of eighteen years, unless otherwise stated by national legislation (United Nations, 1989). There is a legal presumption that anyone under age eighteen lacks competence and the cognitive abilities and mental processes required for knowing, judging, and evaluating (Daly, 2022). The concept, originating from Piaget's (1952) developmental psychology, posits a division between child development based on age and biologically predisposed capabilities, suggesting that children progress through hierarchical stages at roughly the same pace as they age. This universal maturational framework, even though it is a rather passive perspective of child development, has provided the first child-centred approach to early childhood research that included children as active participants in their own learning.

In contrast, a socio-constructivist perspective takes into consideration the quality and nature of children's context, biological development, and cultural and life experiences, and positions children as active agents in their development. Adopting a sociocultural perspective and a child-centred approach, Vygotsky (1978) proposed that children's development is informed by their active participation in the cultural values and beliefs of their community, and via interactions with more knowledgeable peers. Vygotsky regarded children as active agents in their development, and he viewed learning as a collective and cultural activity that happened within a community, via cultural tools (the child's internal thinking processes). Vygotsky connected the social and mental processes in order to describe child development. Like Piaget, Vygotsky too implied that children progress towards adulthood in a universal manner, thus ignoring the fact that diverse factors can affect child development and their lived experiences.

Children's competencies, interests, and abilities may vary widely, irrespective of age. According to Article 5 of the UNCRC, parents and other responsible adults are entrusted with the responsibility of guiding children to exercise their rights 'in a manner consistent with the evolving capabilities of the child'. This means that children under age eighteen can still exercise their rights as they age, and gain experience, but they may need to be supported to do so (Daly, 2020). Set against the backdrop of children's rights, this Element adopts the term 'child' as a unifying term that refers to individuals under eight years of age, who have the ability, capacity, and right to a voice, thus recognising their right to meaningful participation in research.

2.2.2 Children

Traditional psychological research was shaped by the understanding of children as a product of development. In developmental psychology, children are presented as en route to become adults (McDonald, 2009), whereby children progress towards adulthood in ages and stages. Despite the rapid advancements in society, inequality continues to deepen, particularly for children experiencing deprivation and experiences of childhood differ widely, and some may stand in stark contrast with each other. A group of children may grow up in secure environments; others may grow up in distressing environments. Hence, children's early experiences can be profoundly different and 'childhood cannot be described as a universal experience, but one that is constructed within specific times, places and contexts' (Danby & Farrell, 2004, p. 38). To understand children's experiences, it is therefore important that we understand the diversity and complexity experienced by children by examining the factors that influence children's lives, and how these evolve over time. The challenge for early childhood researchers is how to capture the diversity, complexity, and unpredictability in young children's experiences in ways that acknowledge children's voices and agency. For a start, by listening to children's voices, researchers acknowledge children's capacity to describe their opinions about issues that are relevant to them.

2.2.3 Childhood

The concept of childhood is as a social construct (James & Prout, 2015). Our understanding of the child is often perceived by our views on the social constructions of childhood (Prout, 2011). Sociocultural theory presents the concept of childhood as a socially constructed phenomenon, indicating that children are able to actively learn via interactions with others within their sociocultural context (Rogoff, 2003). In fact, cross-cultural, anthropological, and ethnographic research shows that children are not passive recipients of knowledge (Prout & James, 1997). Rather, child development is a socially mediated process that is influenced by the sociocultural influences present in the child's context, drawing attention to the wider environment the child is situated in, and its social, cultural, historical, and political conditions, bringing about a new conceptual shift towards a sociology of childhood (Vygotsky, 1978). In recent years, the New Sociology of Childhood (see Section 3.1) emerged as an attempt to address the gaps in early childhood research concerning children's learning by looking at child development from a historical and cultural lens. Contemporary theories of childhood that have emerged in the New Sociology of Childhood paradigm have opened space for researchers to reflect on the historical, social, and cultural variations in the construction of children and childhood. As a new way of understanding children and childhood, this paradigm shift has opened new avenues in early childhood education research taking into account children's multiple experiences, views, and voices. As a result, in recent years there has been a proliferation of research that directly involves young children and their views. New and creative methods to involve and consult with children have been established, aimed at involving children as participants and experts in their own lives, and as co-researchers. Yet in early childhood studies, the use of diverse methods to listen to children's voices still raises questions related to the relationship between the chosen research methodology, methods, and the theoretical framework underpinning the study. Such questions call for a consideration of the ethical dilemmas that may be present in research involving children, which will be discussed in the next section.

2.3 Concluding Comments

Taking the aforementioned into consideration, this Element recognises that as a social construct, a child, and childhood can be viewed differently across contexts and cultures, and that the chronological age is not a universal marker of the transition into adulthood. Additionally, this Element draws on approaches in psychology, sociology, and anthropology to understand the dominant narratives concerning children and childhood, and education. Consequently, it recognises that children have a right to a voice, a recognition that has given rise to a new discourse around children and childhood and an increase in participatory research with children.

3 Theoretical Perspectives

Section 2 has shown how in recent decades, the theoretical tenets of postmodernism, poststructuralism, and post-foundationalism have helped to create a critical reflection on our understanding of the child, children, and childhood. In this section, we examine the different theoretical perspectives that emerged over time and that aim to encourage young children's meaningful participation in research. The work of Foucault (1975), for example, has profoundly impacted the way we look at knowledge, truth, and power as a form of social control, and the impact of these on the research participants. As such, Foucault's poststructuralist framework provides a lens to explore how children participate in research in ways that acknowledge their voices and agency by taking into consideration the different truths and meanings present in their lives. The aim here is not to debate the different theoretical framework at great lengths – the space in this Element does not allow for that. Rather, what is essential is the understanding that different theoretical frameworks commonly used in early childhood research challenge us to think about research from the different perspectives that underpin children's worldviews. Different theoretical frameworks call for different methodologies, and researchers working with children, seeking to observe the children's world and understand the factors that are present in children's lives, need to be aware of children's voices, capacity, and agency.

3.1 The UNCRC and the New Sociology of Childhood

There have been a number of declarations recognising the rights that all human beings are entitled to. One of the declarations recognising children's rights for protection, freedom, voices, and participation is the United Nations Convention on the Rights of the Child [UNCRC] (United Nations, 1989). The UNCRC is the world's most widely ratified treaty related to children's rights, regardless of their age, abilities, gender, religion, language, or ethnicity. The UNCRC is ratified by all countries worldwide, except the United States of America. Since 1989, the UNCRC has promoted global action upon which local and international legislations are based, and has strongly influenced the ways in which children are consulted and listened to. The UNCRC provides the context in which this Element is based. Respecting children's voices and agency is at the heart of what this Element seeks to achieve *with* and *for* children. Such an approach requires the adoption of a vision that places children's voices and agency at the core of its endeavour.

With the advent of the UNCRC, children's participatory rights have become central, affording children opportunities to communicate their views in a variety of ways in accordance with their age and maturity (Templeton et al., 2023), recognising their agency and capabilities (Coyne et al., 2021; UN Committee on the Rights of the Child, 2009). Current sociological perspectives focus on the concept of children's agency and socialisation as a theoretical perspective introduced by the New Sociology of Childhood studies (Prout, 2011; Tisdall & Punch, 2012). As an alternative paradigm, the New Sociology of Childhood positions children as capable individuals within the research process (Koller & Murphy, 2022). The New Sociology of Childhood focuses on the understanding of children and childhood in diverse cultures and contexts, encouraging the emergence of new research methods in early childhood research. Together, the emergence of the New Sociology of Childhood (Tisdall, 2010; Tisdall & Punch, 2012) and the UNCRC (United Nations, 1989) set the stage for new opportunities to research involving young children that require the use of diverse methods. In turn, the New Sociology of Childhood led to a re-evaluation of children's role in research, with researchers viewing children as active (rather than passive) participants and co-constructors of the research process.

In the last three decades, there has been growing interest by early childhood researchers to recognise children's knowledge, experience, and values, thus recognising children as experts in their own lives, and supporting their participation right in research (Flewitt, 2022; Tisdall & Cuevas-Parra, 2022; United Nations, 1989). Furthermore, the international children's rights movement asserts children's rights in voicing their opinions in matters that concern them (Koller & Murphy, 2022; United Nations, 1989). As a result, researchers moved from conducting research *on* children toward conducting research *with* children, positioning children as interpreters of their own experiences rather than as informants in research (Barratt Hacking et al., 2013; Dockett et al., 2017). The philosophical shift towards viewing children as social agents in their own lives and their active participation in early childhood education and care programmes has increased the importance of listening to children's voices in research, particularly about issues that matter to them. In this context, children are viewed as contributing members of society and as experts on their own lives. Their competence as capable of holding and sharing their own views and opinions is also recognised, and children's views are given serious consideration in research.

As a framework, the UNCRC (United Nations, 1989) is not without its limitations. The UNCRC is considered to be radical and innovative in that it recognises children as social actors and has brought about changes in legislation, policy, and research, yet challenges to children's participation in research remain (Tisdall & Cuevas-Parra, 2022). The UNCRC has been criticised for its lack of consideration of cultural diversity and for allowing governments to cherry-pick specific articles to include in policies, while ignoring others (Urbina-Garcia et al., 2021).

Nowadays, children are more involved in the decision-making of the research process, including deciding upon the objectives, research questions, methods, and analysis of the data, and the evaluation of the dissemination process. Consequently, child-centred research methods that are sensitive to children's needs and contexts, and that recognise the diversity of childhoods in different countries and sociocultural contexts, help children's voices to emerge in meaningful ways.

3.2 Voice

In order to understand what voice means in the context of early childhood, it is important to be cognisant of the notions of children's voices. The UNCRC is often discussed in terms of its focus on the protection, provision, and participation of children (United Nations, 1989). The elements of protection and provision are related to adults' responsibilities towards children; whereas children's participation is related to their voice. Voice is a political act that implies engagement and participation. As clearly stated in Article 12, the UNCRC gives children a right to a voice in matters that affect them (United Nations, 1989). This right is both provocative and problematic because participation is wide in scope and political in nature, and many issues concern children. As such, it is important that children are introduced to the practices of participation early on in order that they may participate in a society as human beings, now and in the future.

The UNCRC does not specifically mention the terms 'voice' or 'voices', but speaks about children's right to be able to express their opinions freely. 'Voice' may be narrowly interpreted as referring only to the spoken voice, but children unable to speak through words can still express their views and, therefore, their voices. Here, 'voices' deliberately refer to the different perspectives of children, an idea derived from the Reggio Emilia Approach with its proposal of the 'hundred languages of children' (Edwards et al., 2011). Therefore, the understanding of children's voices in this Element goes beyond the articulation of words, phrases, or sentences. This is not to suggest that young children have opinions about complex issues that may be beyond them. Rather, it suggests that children have opinions about issues that are of concern to them and that matter to them the most, such as the early childhood contexts they attend and friendship, and adults need to listen to children's voices and act on these appropriately. Given their tender age, children have had fewer experiences of participation than adults, but they are still capable and competent to think for themselves, particularly in matters affecting them. Article 12 recognises that not all children may have similar experiences and capabilities to participate; therefore, it proposes that children's voices be 'given due weight according to the age and maturity of the child' (United Nations, 1989, p. 5). Yet, without proper testing, identifying children's maturity of thought can also be problematic. Perhaps, this is why very young children and non-verbal children are sometimes denied opportunities to express their voices.

3.3 Capacity

In contrast to early childhood education and care, the field of early childhood research has a relatively shorter history that started to emerge slightly over a century ago, but it has changed considerably over time. In this Element, I explain early childhood research as storytelling (File et al., 2017). My intention here is not to draw analogies between research and stories, but to encourage the readers to think about the value of comprehensible stories in an attempt to make the research more meaningful and comprehensible to the audience. Stories offer this potential. Hence, early childhood research tells a story about children's voices about an issue that matters to them.

Traditional sociological perspectives examined childhood as children internalising the world of adulthood. Consequently, research was conducted *on* children, who were considered as passive participants in adult-led research. As a result of the political, theoretical, and methodological diversity that emerged following the publication of the UNCRC (United Nations, 1989), children's participation in research flourished. Internationally, the UNCRC is regarded as the foundation for children's relationships with adults, granting them rights across a range of areas that matter to them, including a right to education, healthy environment, healthcare, play, protection from harm, and privacy. Within this international framework of children's rights, Article 12 states that (a) States Parties shall assure to the child who is capable of forming his or her own views the right to express those views freely in all matters affecting the child, the views of the children being given due weight in accordance with the age and maturity of the child; and (b), for this purpose, the child shall in particular be provided the opportunity to be heard in any judicial and administrative proceedings affecting the child, either directly, or through a representative or an appropriate body, in a manner consistent with the procedural rules of national law.

The recommendations of Article 12 apply to both the individual and the collective, that is, the individual child and groups of children. In sum, Article 12 has given children a right to express their views, have a voice in research and in matters that concern them, and have these taken seriously (United Nations, 1989). This historical moment has uprooted children's dependence on adults for protection and guidance and created a re-conceptualisation of children as social agents, capable of making informed decisions about political, social, and economic issues that affect them (Prout, 2005).

Since the publication of the UNCRC, there has been a large volume of published studies describing children as active agents or actors in their own lives (James et al., 1998; Qvortrup, 2006). Viewing children as having agency acknowledges that they are capable of voicing their opinions. Yet, children's agency is not synonymous to parents or caregivers. The imbalance of power between children and adults should not diminish children's visibility and participation (Daly, 2020). Rather, the recognition of children as actors in society acknowledges their agency. Such recognition requires adults to relinquish some of their power to children, an act some adults may find challenging particularly in a context where adults are also gatekeepers, such as parents and teachers. Caution needs to be exercised when considering the binary view of adult–child power imbalances as it may imply that children's agency is only afforded in relation to adult agency, therefore failing to recognise the complexities involved in power relationships. Rather than focusing on a binary view, this

Elements highlights the idea of children as interacting with others (e.g., researchers). Therefore, this Element provides insights into the diverse research methods currently used in early childhood research to listen to young children's voices and acknowledge their agency.

3.4 Participation

Young children are active agents and contributors of their world. The steady growth of research into young children's lives reveals that when children are given the opportunity to voice their opinions and perspectives, they are capable of doing so as long as researchers use the appropriate research methods. For a number of years, the implementation of the agency theory in research involving children's experiences and perspectives has been questioned, particularly in relation to how children can participate in research as competent actors. In recent years, studies have demonstrated that young children are capable of voicing valuable opinions and they are increasingly listened to (Sun et al., 2023). Yet, they are still not represented in many arenas of life (Lundy, 2007), and further effort to promote their participation is required (Sun et al., 2023). The term 'participation' is used in conjunction with Article 12 of the UNCRC to indicate children's rights and the mutual dialogue and respect between children and adults (Tisdall & Cuevas-Parra, 2022). Even though the term 'participation' is not included in the UNCRC, the overarching premise of the framework is children's participation rights in research, policy, legislations, and practices that include and matter to them (Blaisdell et al., 2022).

Listening to children's voices is an iterative and continuous process that goes beyond individual utterances. Rather, children's meaningful participation in research is a way of listening to their voices. Participation in research is far from perfect and issues with children's participation in research remain nonetheless. Despite the advancements in early childhood research towards conceptualising children as competent social actors and experts in their own lives, there is still the tendency for researchers to view childhood from an adult perspective, 'from a "looking down" standpoint' (Flewitt, 2022, p. 209). Sometimes young children's voices continue to have limited influence on decision-making and policy, especially since adults are the guardians of this right, ultimately judging children based on their age and maturity levels (Templeton et al., 2023).

In an attempt to overcome issues with children's participation in research, Lundy (2007) proposes a model for children's participation. Lundy's participation model asserts that voice is not enough for meaningful participation. She adds that for meaningful engagement with Article 12 of the UNCRC, children also need 'space', 'influence', and 'audience'. Children require suitable information to support the uninhibited expression of their voices, opinions, and perspectives; space where they are safely given the opportunity to express their opinions and views; an audience that actively listens to their ideas and acts upon them; and influence to ensure that adults take children's views seriously and act upon them, where appropriate. These four elements of the Lundy model of children's participation ensure that children's voices are heard within diverse sociocultural contexts. Lundy's model also implies commitment from adults to children's empowerment, a view that entails a political stance from adults who acknowledge their desire to share power with children and make room for children to communicate their ideas. Lundy's model is flexible and fluid, and can be applied to any form of participation for all children in research and other areas of decision-making. Thus far, this model has contributed to ensuring that children are involved in meaningful ways in research and decision-making that affect their lives.

Acknowledgement of children's participation in research requires that adults pay attention to where power lies in relation to children's voices, how that power is enacted, by whom that power is enacted, and what happens to children's voices once expressed. The issue draws on discussion about the power dynamics between children and adults, and entails serious considerations as to how power in adult–child relationships is mediated, and whose voices may be dominant at different times. Listening to children's voices requires adults to be open to new ideas and suggestions from children. In the democratic spirit of children's rights, listening to children's voices also requires that adults are transparent, open, and honest in that they acknowledge the power imbalances that exist at different times during a research process. Power dynamics may change as children grow and their ideas change. To allow children to grow and flourish requires that their voices are nurtured and acted upon.

Set against the backdrop of children's rights, research approaches to listening to children's voices as opposed to regarding them as mini adults have become mainstream, leading to the development of a new discourse influenced by a broad range of research methods (Bradbury-Jones et al., 2018). The concept of giving children a voice in research is described as a social and cultural construct, with arguments by Urbina-Garcia et al. (2021) suggesting that the term 'voices' can occasionally imply 'tokenistic attempts' (p. 2). The difficulties associated with tokenistic participation, such as children having minimal influence on decision-making, the inclusion of select groups while excluding others, and the absence of sustainability, continuity, and accountability, are elucidated by some scholars as well (Lundy, 2007; Tisdall & Cuevas-Parra, 2022). Yet children's participation in research is not a gift from adults to children; rather, it is the right of children (Lundy, 2007). Tokenism can be avoided by ensuring children's meaningful engagement in research, even when adults feel uncomfortable to seek children's views (Lundy, 2007). Tokenism can also be avoided by not treating children as a homogenous group, an action which could potentially further undermine and oppress children, but rather seeking children's voices in ways that empower them. These are significant issues that call for a better understanding of children's agency in research, ethics, relationships, consent, and assent.

3.5 Ethics

Ethics is a central dimension to all research involving children. Ethical research is guided by ethical goals and values that 'are integrated with the efforts undertaken out of respect, interest and appreciation of the diverse others who are our research participants and audiences' (Gilliat-Ray et al., 2022, p. 90). In early childhood research in particular, researchers are expected to uphold high ethical standards. Formal ethical guidelines such as the British Research Association Ethical Guidelines for Educational Research [BERA] (2018), the European Early Childhood Educational Research Association [EECERA] (Bertam et al., 2015), and the WMA Declaration of Helsinki (2022) are often referred to as the gold standard of guiding ethical behaviour and decision-making for researchers. Further legal ethical requirements may be in place to protect participants and researchers during the research process in specific contexts. One such example is the General Data Protection Regulation [GDPR] (European Union, 2016), which is a legal requirement designed to ensure data privacy across Europe and to protect citizens' rights to know who, why and when their personal data are being stored, accessed, and used.

Regardless of how rigorous ethical guidelines may be, researchers will almost inevitably face ethical challenges throughout the research process. Universal ethical guidelines are helpful, however, when researchers need to manage certain ethical dilemmas in practice; such guidelines may turn out to be challenging because of the multiple influences that shape both participants and researchers. Dealing with ethical dilemmas requires researchers to weigh the pros and cons of each outcome before applying ethical principles in practice. Nevertheless, it is paramount that researchers develop a clear understanding of the ethical principles that guide early childhood research and then engage in critical reflection to respond appropriately to any ethical challenges that may arise at all stages during the research process. The aim is to listen to children's voices in inclusive and positive ways, where children feel respected, safe, and confident to participate in the research. Researchers need to strike a balance between ethical design of the research and their values and the safety and well-being of the children they will be working with. The key is to develop an ethical framework that enables the researchers to address the research questions while eliminating the risk of harm to the participants. A robust and well-grounded ethical framework is likely to help guide the researchers in the decision-making process.

Yet research ethics is complex, and multiple factors shape ethically planned research and decision-making. One of the complexities lies in the fact that research is largely influenced by local culture, politics, and traditions, and therefore, there are variations between ethical guidelines and the way these are enacted in different contexts, and the way children are conceptualised as knowledgeable individuals. Irrespective of these differences, the UNCRC remains the most recognised set of established international guiding principles for children's rights to a voice.

Critiques of universal codes of ethics remain. Ethical guidelines are open to interpretation, and therefore, they can be misinterpreted or misused at international, national, or local levels. Regardless, ethical guidelines remain necessary and their review processes ensure that such ethics create space for fair decision-making for all (children and researchers) during the research process.

3.6 Relationships

Given the fast growth of the research base with children as co-researchers in the past three decades, children's perspectives have been foregrounded. Early childhood research is underpinned by the belief that adult–child relationships are reciprocal and equally important. Relationships, respect, and reciprocity are key to gaining access to children's insights. Trusting and respectful relationships develop over time via listening with all the senses (Rinaldi, 2021). Establishing trusting relationships when conducting research with young children takes time so that children understand what the research is about and what it entails (Fleet & Harcourt, 2018). Strong and healthy relationships based on trust and mutual respect can profoundly impact the outcomes of the research process. This is the case in all kinds of research but is particularly so in early childhood research where researchers often build close associations with child participants and their communities, often for an extended period of time. Establishing trust is a time-consuming effort, yet it is important that the research process is built on trust between children and researchers. As adults, researchers are responsible to safeguard children by learning about, and developing respect for, the children's community, culture, interests, and needs, and protect their privacy. The time invested in building trusting relationships will reap benefits for the well-being of all involved.

In early childhood research, the asymmetry in the power relations between adult researchers and children cannot be completely eliminated (Fleet & Harcourt, 2018). The relationship between the researchers and the children, and respect for children's voices, may present ethical challenges. Protecting privacy can be particularly challenging when research is conducted in small and tight-knit communities. In such circumstances, when researchers feel that there is a conflict of interest in place, researchers must adhere to ethical standards and take ethical decisions that respect the participants' rights and interests before their own. Several ethical challenges are involved when addressing power imbalances between adults and children in research. For a start, recognising that power differences could exist when conducting research with children already signifies an understanding of children's agency. Issues of assent and/or consent from children, children's age, collaboration, cooperation, and co-research may present several challenges to researchers. Over time, a number of these challenges have generated an ongoing debate around their perplexity.

Another challenge faced by researchers when conducting research with young children is due to the fact that some children may find it difficult to convey their ideas in words. Therefore, in such situations, researchers use methodologies that empower children's authentic and active participation, where the imbalance of power between adult researchers and child participants can be minimised.

3.7 Consent and Assent

When conducting research, children, parents, and caregivers need to be informed about the intent of the research before they agree to participate. Ensuring that participants are given appropriate information about the research at every stage of the research process is a crucial part of the research design (Bishop, 2014; Bradbury-Jones et al., 2018; Fleet & Harcourt, 2018; Sun et al., 2023). Since adults hold the legal right to make decisions about children's participation in research, parental or caregiver consent should always be sought to ensure the participants' willingness to be involved in the research continues.

It is common practice for researchers to seek permissions from several education authorities before being allowed to conduct research with children. Seeking formal institutional consent is the first step. Gaining signed consent from parents or caregivers, followed by the children's assent is the next step in the research process. As gatekeepers, parents, teachers, and administrators are likely to seek reassurance about the research to make sure that young children are not exposed to harm. Researchers hold a moral responsibility to effectively communicate the research procedures as participants frequently base their understanding of consent on the information provided about the research process.

Consent falls within the jurisdiction of adults, and there is no legal foundation for ensuring that children are adequately informed (O'Farrelly & Tatlow-Golden, 2022). Establishing children's informed consent is generally framed as assent (Lahman, 2018; Lundy, 2007). Assent refers to the agreement of individuals lacking legal capacity to provide consent for engagement in an activity (O'Farrelly & Tatlow-Golden, 2022). Assent is a form of verbal consent and is not as legally binding as adult consent, but it demonstrates respect for the child as a person. In contexts involving children or adults lacking decision-making capacity, consent from a parent or legal guardian alongside assent from the individual is necessary for participation. Assent cannot be solely relied upon to safeguard the child; parental consent or permission serves as the primary protective measure. Therefore, it is crucial to interpret assent only in conjunction with parental/caregiver consent (Miller & Nelson, 2006). In this Element, assent is positioned as a process of involving children in decision-making about their participation in research, therefore recognising their competencies and agency.

Gaining informed consent from very young children can be problematic as they may not have a clear understanding of what research is and how their assent may impact them. When granting assent, children should not be subjected to identical informal and decision-making criteria as adults providing informed consent (Roth-Cline & Nelson, 2013). Researchers may benefit from tools to support children's assent in research about their lives (O'Farrelly & Tatlow-Golden, 2022). Employing a process of documentation to secure children's informed consent not only respects their autonomy but also serves to enhance their communicative abilities (Fleet & Harcourt, 2018). When conducting research with young children, researchers may start by exploring the concept of 'research' with children – asking children what research means to them, showing them recording equipment and how it is used in research, and how the research is presented in the form of an illustrated book (Spiteri, 2016). Young children are encouraged to handle the illustrated book and other research materials presented to them. Researchers may even plan activities with the children in which children try out research methods together before they are asked for their assent. Once researchers are sure that the children have understood what the research process entails, they can seek initial assent. Assent is often sought in the presence of a witness (an adult) and the participant verbally agrees to participate in the study. The witness is often chosen by the children rather than the researchers (Lahman, 2018).

Children's right to assent in research allows them the right to withhold assent, that is, the right to withdraw from the study without declaring why (Lahman, 2018; O'Farrelly & Tatlow-Golden, 2022; Spiteri, 2016). Seeking children's assent is an ongoing process in that children's participation in research is constantly negotiated and re-negotiated. Children's understanding of assent is frequently revisited during the research process, not only to support children's memories but also to help them understand what happened before and what will happen next, and to remind them that they can opt in or out of the research at any time without any consequences. It is suggested that when conducting research with young children, researchers are mindful of children's non-verbal cues, indicating their (un)willingness to continue as participants throughout the study. This means that children have a right refuse to participate in research even if their parents/caregivers have consented to their participation, particularly in instances when they show discomfort during the research process.

An emphasis on children's right to agency is addressed via assent and an understanding of the role and responsibilities of the researchers (O'Farrelly & Tatlow-Golden, 2022), which requires a reflexive stance. Researchers have the moral responsibility to ensure that children have a clear understanding of what the research process entails, what will happen to the information that researchers gather about them, and reassure children that it is fine to withdraw from the research altogether. Researchers bring their past experiences to the research process and learning during the research process happens based on their past experiences. Reflexivity, or what is sometimes referred to as intersubjectivity, requires a process of self-reflection of the ways in which the researchers and their role, intentions, and methods can influence the participants and the researchers' own assumptions (Flewitt & Ang, 2020; Lahman, 2018). In early childhood research, reflexivity entails an examination of the intersubjective relationships between the researchers and the children, and how meaning is co-constructed through dialogue as a result of these relationships (Flewitt & Ang, 2020).

3.8 Anonymity and Confidentiality

Issues around anonymity and confidentiality pervade all stages of the research process. Researchers are to negotiate with the children the degree of anonymity required, which may vary depending on the population, research aims and questions and the intended avenues of the findings. Some participants may prefer complete anonymity; others may prefer to be identified. Each of these scenarios presents researchers with different ethical dilemmas. Solutions to issues of anonymity and confidentiality will depend on the ethical requirements of the legal and institutional requirements involved in the research process, the kind of data collected and the population involved.

Ensuring anonymity in audio-recorded data, for example, is relatively easy because the identity of the participants can be concealed, especially since audio-recorded data are often presented as transcribed extracts. The transcripts are sent to participants for verification before the data are analysed. At this stage, participants are free to make changes to their data. Visual data such as photographs can be more challenging to anonymise because while certain images can be blurred/smudged, the technical equivalent of anonymising written text, others cannot. The process of anonymising visual data can be time-consuming and costly. For this reason, visual data such as drawings are often used in research with young children to protect children's privacy and identity. Drawings carry the advantage of participant anonymity, yet they may be difficult for researchers to 'read'. Therefore, children's drawings are often accompanied by an interview, during which the children explain the significance of their drawing to the researchers (Spiteri, 2020).

Participant anonymity and confidentiality are important to uphold in any research. Yet, occasionally, researchers are legally obliged to pass on information acquired during the research process, for example, for child protection purposes. It is, therefore, advisable to include a clause in the consent sheet given to adults and older children to let them know that reporting of child safety may be required.

3.9 Concluding Comments

Children's rights to meaningful participation in research raise important questions about how adults who conduct research with children prioritise children's well-being in the research process. Research ethics are paramount in research that listens to children's voices and acknowledges their agency. Ethics are influenced by multiple factors such as international, national, and local ethical guidelines, and these may differ between countries. Regardless of how different the ethical requirements may be, it is almost certain the researchers will need to negotiate and re-negotiate the ethical dilemmas that may arise throughout the research process. The key here is to develop a robust and well-grounded ethical framework that enables researchers to engage in ethical research practices and guide their decision-making, and one in which the risk of harm to children is eliminated.

4 Quantitative Research in Early Childhood

This section introduces quantitative and child-centred research methods that afford children voice and agency in research, and a description of the characteristics associated with these. To this end, this section explores the relation between positivist research, quantitative methodology, and the use of experimental methods in early childhood research. It delves into the debate surrounding the use of experimental research and randomised controlled trials (RCTs) in early childhood education research, and explores the differing perspectives on what constitutes scientific research and the debates in the field. The aim here is to explain the basic principles of conducting early childhood research in the quantitative paradigm and to cover several key methods used in quantitative research, while addressing ethical considerations regarding the use of experimental and randomised trial approaches in early childhood research. This section also explores the implications of quantitative methodological approaches for early childhood education research, practice, and policy development, and gaps in the field.

4.1 Quantitative Research with Young Children

Rooted in the positivist paradigm, quantitative research follows the scientific method, and uses a deductive approach to testing theories and hypotheses (Bryman & Bell, 2019). A quantitative approach to research is used to seek an explanation of the natural world through observation and/or experimentation, and a collection of empirical/measurable data. Traditionally, early childhood research has been characterised as being objective in nature and it primarily focused on quantitative methods to collect data, including experimental designs, observations, and questionnaires. Current quantitative research tends to align with the post-positivist paradigm (Harrison & Wang, 2018). Post-positivism acknowledges the idea of objective truth. Post-positivism also acknowledges that the discovery of reality is limited to certain probability, and accepts the fact that the positionality of the researchers can influence what is being observed and measured (Bryman & Bell, 2019).

There is growing recognition that young children express their views in a variety of ways, not limited to drawings or verbal communication only. In fact, high-quality, large-scale quantitative research using deductive approaches to test theories and hypotheses is increasing in early childhood research. Indeed, in recent years, there has been a demand for high-quality, large-scale quantitative studies in research in relation to the effects of early childhood education, the impact of intervention programmes, and children's learning and development (Harrison & Wang, 2018). Such studies have been used to design and justify policy, curricula and provision in the early years (Flewitt & Ang, 2020). Nevertheless, how children express their voices in quantitative research is limited. The questions remain as to whether we can use scientific methods to conduct research with children, and if so, how we can listen to children in such a way that their voices and agency are asserted in research, and are taken seriously by adults.

4.2 Experimental Research

Experimental research, rooted in the positivist paradigm and the natural sciences, emerged during the European Renaissance and Enlightenment. It emphasises empirical evidence, rigorous experimentation, and control of variables to establish causality, and aims to establish causality by deliberately controlling and manipulating conditions to observe the effects on variables. It typically begins with a hypothesis, followed by designing and conducting experiments, evaluating results, and accepting or rejecting the hypothesis. Experimental research focuses on distinguishing between facts, describing 'what is', and values, which involve moral judgements about 'what ought to be'.

Researchers manipulate the independent variable and observe changes in the dependent variable. In laboratory settings, variables can be tightly controlled, but in naturalistic environments, quasi-experimental methods are often used due to limitations in control. Experimental research emphasises systematic processes and statistical methods to ensure precision and minimise bias. Researchers aim to isolate the effects of the independent variable by controlling other variables and randomly assigning participants to groups. Through systematic observation and measurement in scientific experiments, the truth or validity of phenomena can be tested, leading to the development of theories based on observable facts. This approach enhances internal validity by attributing any differences between groups to the independent variable, rather than external factors or biases. Experimental research asserts that truth can be reliably known through experimentation and measurement, with objectivity characterising the research process to avoid subjective bias (Flewitt & Ang, 2020).

Experimental research in early childhood education has a rich history dating back to the late nineteenth century, marked by the development of child psychology. Early researchers advocated for meticulous experimental methods to study child behaviour and development (Thorpe, 1946). These methods, including controlled experiments and objective tests, were seen as pioneering despite their challenges. Throughout history, experimental techniques have been used to predict, monitor, and assess various aspects of child development, emotional development, and behaviours. Experimental research has also played a significant role in evaluating early childhood education programmes and interventions, such as the 'Lasting Effects of Early Education' (Lazar et al., 1982), in the United States, and the 'Sure Start', in the UK (Melhuish et al., 2008). Overall, experimental research in early childhood education continues to provide valuable insights into the effectiveness of interventions and programmes, helping to improve the educational experiences and outcomes of young children worldwide (Flewitt & Ang, 2020).

Even though experimental methods have yielded significant advances in the natural sciences, most policymakers and empirical scientists acknowledge limitations to the conclusions that can be drawn from the approach but do not agree with efforts to curtail its use.

4.3 Variable-Oriented and Person-Oriented Approaches

Quantitative research tests hypotheses by controlling and modifying variables. Quantitative research is described as the study of the relation between variables represented in numeric forms (Harrison & Wang, 2018), where the relation between variables is tested through statistical analysis (File et al., 2017). There are two types of variable-centred analysis: *parametric* (used to examine the relation among variables) and *non-parametric* tests (used for the examination of nominal or ordinal data). In quantitative research, variables that, when measured, indicate an equivalent or increased measurable value, thus being more precise, are called continuous or interval variables (e.g., age, income, education). Continuous variables are created from questionnaires and surveys. A variable-centred approach to early childhood research can explain the differences between groups of children. Here, the focus is on an 'average' population for which findings are generalised. The focus on an average population is a limitation of variable-oriented approach in quantitative research.

In the literature, a person-oriented analysis is presented as an alternative approach to a variable-oriented approach. In a person-oriented approach, the focus is on the relationship between participants rather than on the relation between variables. A person-oriented methodological approach to quantitative research takes into account the complexity of human behaviour (Harrison & Wang, 2018). Person-oriented approaches include cluster analysis, latent class analysis, and growth mixture modelling. A person-oriented approach has been criticised for its lack of appeal and endorsement by developmental scholars, and for the confusion it creates (Laursen, 2015). There are two types of confusions that characterise a person-oriented approach (Laursen, 2015). The first confusion is a semantic one, and lies in the overlap and incorrect use of the term. Some use the terms 'person-centred' to mean 'person-oriented' concurrently and interchangeably. Both terms (person-centred and person-oriented) focus on the individual, but a person-oriented approach emphasises the holistic understanding of the individual. A person-centred approach is interactional. The second confusion stems from the false assertion that qualitative research is person-oriented research, which is not the case. Other challenges included lack of software to analyse person-oriented research. As a developmental scholar, Laursen (2015) suggests that rather than viewing the person-oriented and variable-oriented approaches as opposites, it is more beneficial for empirical research to join the two techniques. In early child-hood research, person-oriented approaches to research are used more often and they help to acknowledge children's voices and agency in research by listening to children's ideas about matters that are significant to them, such as friendships. Still, more research is required in the field particularly with very young children such as infants and toddlers.

4.4 Randomised Control Trials

Randomised controlled trials are a form of experimental research where parti-cipants are randomly assigned to different groups to test interventions. Randomised controlled trials and experimental and quasi-experimental studies are often considered the 'gold-standard' methodologies by policymakers for enhancing policy development, especially in education and the broader social sciences (Flewitt & Ang, 2020). Random assignment of participants is crucial but can be challenging in naturalistic settings (see Section 4.5). Following the random assignment of participants, pre-tests and post-tests are used to assess the effects of interventions on experimental groups compared to control groups.

There is debate over the hierarchy of evidence, with RCTs being strong in internal validity but weaker in external validity compared to quasi-experimental methods. Critics argue against conceptualising methodologies in a hierarchy, advocating for matching research questions to specific types of research instead (Flewitt & Ang, 2020). Yet policymakers are likely to favour experimental designs because they provide evidence-based research and practice, and are driven by a contemporary neoliberal quest for accountability (Flewitt & Ang, 2020). Despite debates in the field, most scholars advocate the use of RCT and quasi-experimental designs jointly, as a way of developing converging evidence and taking advantages of the strengths of each approach (Gerholm Kallioinen et al., 2019; White & Sabarwal, 2014). These methodologies are preferred for their robustness and trustworthiness in establishing causal findings (Gopalan et al., 2020; White & Sabarwal, 2014).

4.5 Identification and Enrolment of Participants

Quantitative research is used to generalise the results to a larger population of participants, leading to a large sample size. Statistical analyses usually require a large number of participants in order to ensure strong statistical analysis of the data. Quantitative studies recruit more participants than qualitative studies. In theory, the large sample size is representative of a larger population of partici-pants. For the results to stand, a carefully chosen and accurate representative sample of the population is studied. A large-enough representative sample can be challenging to achieve because participation in research is based on the participants' willingness to voluntarily participate in a study. As such, locating a large number of participants for a study for sample sizes to be formed as desired by researchers can be difficult. In such instances, researchers rely on convenience sampling that is reflective of the most suitable arrangements possible for any given population, at any given time (File et al., 2017).

An important aspect of early childhood research is the identification and description of naturalistic groups and subgroups of children in terms of specific characteristics. The identification of these characteristics is important as it helps researchers in designing more targeted interventions (Harrison & Wang, 2018). Groups and subgroups of children can be identified in a variety of ways. For example, they could be identified by gender and language(s) spoken. Identification methods may include direct testing of children's abilities, such as language skills. Based on these outcomes, children are then grouped into categories, for example, gifted or typical development.

4.6 Ways of Listening to Young Children's Voices in Experimental Research

In the past, proxy reporting of children's subjective viewpoints was employed in quantitative research with children, who were rarely included in surveys and questionnaires because young children were often considered incapable of providing reliable and valid data. Nowadays, early childhood research has moved towards a more agentic view of children. In fact, children are now considered to be the best respondents for their own subjective opinions. Accordingly, attention in quantitative research has shifted towards acknowledging children's rights to a voice.

In experimental research, researchers measure an interesting phenomenon they study via numerical data, highlighting the importance of the instruments and measures chosen to collect data – a complex and important part of the research study. In the following section, we will delve into various quantitative methods that researchers can employ to listen to the voices of young children and recognise their agency within quantitative research methodologies.

4.6.1 Surveys and Questionnaires

Researchers are increasingly positioning young children as experts in their own lives and more quantitative research is being conducted with young children, predominantly surveys. The challenge for understanding the best-practices in surveying young children remains, with literacy being one of the major issues encountered when administering surveys to children before age eight (Roni et al., 2020). To support young children's voices and agency in quantitative research, surveys for young children use simple, succinct language and do not contain complex or double and leaning questions (Roni et al., 2020). Of course, this does not mean that children under age eight cannot participate in quantitative research. What this implies is that researchers need to employ creative ways of surveying children in the early years that are suitable for the children's cognitive development and their ability to respond to the questions, keeping in mind that developmental differences among children may influence their understanding and perception of survey questions. Despite their utility, surveys are subject to various limitations. These encompass factors such as a potentially low response rate, which hinges on participants' willingness to engage and their honesty. Additionally, the level of structure in surveys might constrain the validity of responses, while questions may overlook crucial variables. Furthermore, the methodology employed can introduce bias into the samples, and respondents may not adequately represent the surveyed population (Greig et al. (2013).

Questionnaires are another popular research tool used with young children. Questionnaires designed specifically for young children include the use of pictures and short, simple sentences (Siagian et al., 2021). Particular attention is required for choosing the appropriate question format, and the organisation of questions in that they need to be easy and relevant to children, contain few simple and concrete words the children are familiar with, and the sentences are simple in structure and do not contain double negatives (Dillman et al., 2014). In order to listen to young children's voices and assert their agency in questionnaires, early childhood researchers use a combination of true or false questions to depict their questions using pictures. In their study with children in grades one through three, Kähler et al. (2020) used questionnaires that included a choice of simple and complex multiple-choice questions in the form of true or false answers, using pictures. Pictures are enjoyed by most children and provide a concrete way for them to understand the questions posed by researchers, thus empowering children to provide meaningful responses.

One way of listening to children as active agents in the research process is for researchers to design surveys and questionnaires with children, acknowledging children's agency. Once questionnaire items have been chosen, researchers can work with children to translate questions into comprehensible language that children in a specific age group and culture can understand. Research shows that including children in the process of creating the questionnaire results in the most optimal and dependable outcomes, thus highlighting the effectiveness of this collaborative approach (Hirosawa & Oga-Baldwin, 2023). More importantly, when working with young children, using a limited number of easy-to-answer questions can lead to the best results. In this way, surveys and questionnaires empower children's voices and acknowledge their agency in quantitative research.

4.6.2 Observations

Another classic example of experimental research is based on the observation of young children (Piaget, 1952). In a manner reminiscent of Piaget's experiments, structured observations are conducted in 'naturalistic' settings, allowing for the observation of children in their everyday environments. Observations present a form of methodological experimentation that reclaims children's agency and voices in quantitative research. In the literature, there are several examples of structured observational techniques used in early childhood research.

Examples of structured observations included researchers situated behind a two-way mirror watching the interactions and behaviours of a parent and a child during free play. Other examples include the target child method, commonly used to observe preschool children, either individually or in groups; and the time sampling approach, which is a method of observing children at fixed intervals, over a long period of time, to study behaviour that is directly observable and unambiguous (Greig et al., 2013). Structured video observations, consisting of two-minute sequences, were employed to observe children's types of play and well-being, as well as to measure how they spent their time in different play environments (Stroli & Hansen Sandseter, 2019). Time sampling observations were also utilised to explore how children (aged three to six years) engaged in different types of play using features in the outdoor environment (Hansen Sandseter et al., 2022). Children were observed in two-minute intervals throughout the day, and observations were video-recorded and conducted according to a strict protocol to ensure the uniformity of observation sequences and data collection methods across different institutions (Hansen Sandseter et al., 2022). Another method of observations used in experimental research is event sampling. In a study with Finnish children with autism (aged 59–85 months), the researchers used systematic event sampling observations. Each child was observed individually by different researchers to explore their everyday learning processes (Syrjämäkia et al., 2023). In another study, with young Australians, the children were offered open-ended play resources to play with for half an hour, with a partner of their choice to explore how children develop language and relationships through play (Hoyte et al., 2015). Next, the children were video-recorded in dyads during play and the researchers stopped recording after half an hour or when the children showed a desire to conclude the play session (Hoyte et al., 2015). A similar study using play dyads was conducted in the United States to explore young children's problem-solving skills during play using video-recorded sessions and play sets (Gold et al., 2022) Even though researchers need to be skilled at recognising triggers of an event or a behaviour, this method provides a better understanding of the dynamics of an event or a behaviour, therefore allowing for better behaviour or event management (Gold et al., 2022; Greig et al., 2013). The checklist method is another structured observation method that is based on a rating scale used to measure the similarities and differences in individual developmental norms. This method is used as a guide to observe children's developmental milestones (Greig et al., 2013; Sheridan, 2008).

In order to generate a large amount of quantifiable data over a short period of time, researchers can use a combination of methods (Greig et al., 2013). One such example is the use of an observational behaviour mapping framework to examine the environmental features of a large natural playscape for young children's outdoor play activities (Loebach & Cox, 2022). Data recording included time sampling and event sampling to collect information about outdoor play type, activity intensity, risk behaviours, and environmental engagement (Loebach & Cox, 2022).

Observations allow children to voice their ideas through play and other modes of communication during social interactions. Yet human observations are limited in their ability to fully grasp the entirety of social interactions in a context (Messinger et al., 2019). Young children may shy away from expressing their thoughts and feelings, or they may not possess the language skills to express their thoughts in words, making it difficult for researchers to understand the spatial organisation of children's interactions. Social interaction between young children can be studied by employing simultaneous continuous measurement, which is another observational approach to data collection (Messinger et al., 2019). Continuous location data between five-year-olds have observed for an hour on three different occasions during free play observations to track young children's location and movements through a commercially available system utilising radio frequency identification (RFID) tracking system (Messinger et al., 2019). The researchers were able to track social interactions to create visual mapping of the classroom network (Messinger et al., 2019). Similarly, RFID tracking systems were used in a longitudinal study to observe reciprocal patterns of peer speech in preschool children with and without hearing loss, showing that children influenced each other's dyadic speech in a reciprocal manner (Perry et al., 2022). In such observations, children can assert their agency through their behaviour and interactions. When children are observed during play for example, they are more in control of their interactions with peers or adults; therefore, the observed behaviour is true to children's voices.

Observations align with the pedagogy proposed by the Reggio Emilia Approach, which focuses on the hundred languages of children, proposing that there are various ways of listening to children (Edwards et al., 2011). Via observations, researchers can listen to children's voices without actually requiring the children to use verbal language skills. Therefore, as research tools in experimental research, observations afford young children a voice and agency in research.

4.6.3 Interviews

Well-designed interviews are a data collection method used in research to listen to young children's voices in order to explore their worldviews. The interactive nature of interviews allows researchers access to information that may not always be retrieved by other means. During interviews, researchers can pick on certain cues when listening to children's voices. Such cues provide researchers with information about what matters the most to young children.

By their very nature, interviews require time and attention to detail. Structured interviews are commonly used in experimental research with young children. Structured interviews are like interactive questionnaires, and are commonly used to collect quantitative data. Structured interviews with young children often take place as conversations. Structured conversations were conducted with children, and an online questionnaire was utilised with the staff members by Sivertsen and Moe (2022) to measure Norwegian children's well-being. During the interview, the children were asked seven questions related to their participation in their institution and all had four possible answers: often, sometimes, almost never and never. As another way of listening to young children's voices in research, interviews can create a trusting and conversational partnership between children and researchers. Even though in structured interviews, probing and prompting is not used, such interviews still afford children agency in the research process and offer another way of listening to children's voices and acknowledge their agency in the research process.

4.6.4 Peer Nomination

Peers provide the context for social learning, such as collaboration and conflict management, early on in life. With a long history in psychological and socio-logical disciplines, peer nomination is used to understand behaviour in social settings from the children's perspectives (Cillessen & Marks, 2017; Marks, 2017). Specifically, peer nomination is a sociometric assessment tool used in developmental research for assessing relationships and friendships (Guimond et al., 2022; Laursen et al., 2023), social networks (DeLay et al., 2021), and interpersonal behaviour (Mehari et al., 2019; Wu et al., 2022) among children by collecting data from peer informants.

Peer nomination is a form of peer informant measure that is used to study peer relations involving three levels – individual, dyadic, and group level. For example, in a standard sociometric assessment, children are asked to nominate peers they like or like least. The number of nominations received for each question is counted and corrected for differences. Continuous scores for both social preferences and impacts are created. Finally, using a set of decision rules, children's scores are classified in a group.

The majority of peer nomination research in the literature involves children between ages two and eighteen years, and has been conducted mostly in school contexts, for example, to identify children at risk and classroom improvement strategies. Wu et al. (2022) report that as a research method, peer nomination has been effective for understanding young children (aged two to six years) prosocial behaviour too.

Peer nomination has received its fair share of criticism, mostly due to concerns about the ethics surrounding children's choices of social behaviour. Other methods, such as peer ratings, could be less harmful than peer nomination (Mehari et al., 2019). Although peer nomination is not a completely objective measure, it has some of the advantages when compared to other methods such as observations because peer nomination is less costly. Peer nomination also allows for the assessment of relationships and behaviour that are difficult to assess during structured or naturalistic observations (Cillessen & Marks, 2017). For peer nomination to be an effective method, the number of meaningful nominations collected from participants needs to be maximised and it needs to include information about the reliability and validity of this sociometric method (Cillessen & Marks, 2017). Indeed, peer nominations have been used for a long time to collect valid and reliable data. Some consider data from nominations to be more accurate than that derived from self-reports. Still, peer nomination is a form of child report, with children acting as active agents capable of voicing their opinions in the research process.

4.7 Critiques of Experimental Research

New approaches to data collection and improvements in analytical tools and techniques are moving the field forward. Quantitative research, with its emphasis on numerical data and statistical analyses, inherently benefits from the rigorous scrutiny facilitated by replication. Indeed, replication is the gold standard for evaluating empirical evidence (Plucker & Makel, 2021). The ability to replicate findings allows for the verification of results across multiple studies, thereby enhancing the robustness and validity of quantitative research outcomes. Together with a strong theoretical foundation, replication not only underscores the reliability of empirical data but also serves as a cornerstone for establishing the credibility and generalisability of research findings across various contexts and populations (Plucker & Makel, 2021).

Yet experimental research in early childhood education has its own limitations and faces critiques regarding validity, politicisation, and ethical considerations (Flewitt & Ang, 2020). Some limitations of experimental research in early childhood include the availability of a large enough sample to meet the requirements of the study and the appropriateness of quantitative methods for collecting data with young children in diverse sociocultural settings (File et al., 2017; Harrison & Wang, 2018). Validity concerns arise due to the complexity of social behaviours and the inability to fully control variables in natural settings, like classrooms (Scott & Usher, 2011), making the measurement of outcomes or cause-and-effect relationships problematic (Flewitt & Ang, 2020).

Children are not a homogenous group, and they behave in ways that may be difficult to isolate by variables alone. As a result, critics argue that experimental designs produce inconsistent and unreliable results, undermining their suitability for social sciences (Scott & Usher, 2011). Some researchers advocate for the objectivity of experimental research, whereas others warn against overlooking the perspectives of education professionals (Flewitt & Ang, 2020). Issues of internal and external validity further complicate the interpretation of research findings. Nevertheless, critics caution against overgeneralising results and emphasise the importance of robust research design and implementation (Flewitt & Ang, 2020; Scott & Usher, 2011).

With its focus on deductive methods to test theories, experimental research has been aligned with cost-benefit models in policy making; however, its funding priorities are also criticised for perpetuating social inequalities (Fleer & van Oers, 2018; Flewitt & Ang, 2020). Critics argue that experimental methods may overlook the unequal opportunities for learning experienced by disadvantaged populations (Flewitt & Ang, 2020). Such criticism calls for ethical responsibility in research. Researchers need to consider the broader social implications of their work and advocate for a combination of experimental and qualitative approaches to provide comprehensive insights into educational phenomena. Ultimately, experimental research should be viewed as one component of a broader research landscape, contributing to a collective understanding of educational issues.

4.8 Concluding Comments

This section detailed quantitative research in early childhood research. Debates persist regarding the nature and methods of experimental research in early childhood education and social sciences. It is crucial for researchers to recognise and appreciate the diversity of methodologies and research practices in early childhood research. Each approach has its strengths and limitations, and the success of research hinges on its application. The reliability of research findings should be based on their relevance to the specific context and their ability to address the intended problem. Ultimately, the suitability of experimental research, RCTs, or any other method depends on the research objectives, the research questions being addressed, the robustness of the research design, and the context in which the findings are applied.

5 Qualitative Research in Early Childhood

This section introduces qualitative research methods and the characteristics associated with these. It explores the question of when children can participate meaningfully in research, challenging the perception of children as too immature to express their views reliably. It also discusses how sociological perspectives have reshaped our understanding of child competence, leading to research considering children as experts in their own lives by tracing the roots of participatory research methods with children to a movement for democratic research, inspired by critical theory. Finally, this section analyses young children's roles in research, and how research methods have been influenced by perceptions of children's competencies and voices. Several international examples are used to illustrate how young children have been actively involved in qualitative research, and how their participation has created impactful research outcomes.

5.1 Qualitative Research with Young Children

Qualitative research is often related to language and text, and is characterised by inductive approaches to data collection. Here, the use of word-based and visual data is highlighted, reminding us of the importance of the different modes of communication as socio-constructivist tools. Qualitative research methods in early childhood research can be varied, and they align well with sociocultural theories, making them very relevant to early childhood research. Within the qualitative paradigm, data are embedded in naturalistic research and are generated rather than collected, requiring constant and detailed attention to ethical decision-making during the research process.

Historically, children have not been credited by adults as competent individuals. Rather, children have been considered as being 'too innocent and/or immature to participate meaningfully' in research (MacNaughton et al., 2008, p. 164). Since the early 1990s, there has been an increased interest in securing children's rights. As a result, initiatives to engage children as active contributors to their own development and their community in research have gained momentum, notably in Western countries (Yamaguchi et al., 2022). Consequently, our awareness of children's participation rights in research has increased, creating a paradigm shift in the use of qualitative methodologies that listen to children's voices and acknowledge their agency.

5.2 Participatory Research

In recent years, there has been a great deal of interest in the field of qualitative research regarding the use of participatory research approaches. Qualitative research is defined as participatory because 'researchers bring data into being: we *make* them. Making data involves inventing, imagining, encountering, and embracing lived experience and material documentation as methodological praxis. Making requires resourcefulness and participation' (Ellingson & Sotirin, 2020, p. 5). Of interest to this Element is qualitative research conducted with young children, with a special focus on participatory research, where children play a significant and equivalent role to adult researchers, and have a right to be involved in some or all stages of the research process – from conception to dissemination (Bishop, 2014; Blaisdell et al., 2022; Bradbury-Jones et al., 2018).

Participation is an ongoing process, which includes 'information-sharing and dialogue between children and adults based on mutual respect, in which children can learn how their views and those of adults are taken into account and shape the outcome of such processes' (UN Committee on the Rights of the Child, 2009, p. 3). Participatory research stems from critical theorists like Freire and Giroux, who collaborated with marginalised communities to research their own lives and instigate collective change. Participatory research, akin to action research, aims for transformative change through active participant engagement. However, it often carries a political agenda, seeking to empower under-represented groups such as young children, the elderly, individuals with disabilities, and those facing social or economic challenges.

Participatory research shifts the focus from researching children to conducting research *with* and *by* children. It emphasises the use of practical and dialogic approaches that generate knowledge collaboratively *with* children rather than extracting knowledge *from* them. This process fosters self-awareness and serves as a catalyst for positive change. Participatory research, typically qualitative, prioritises involving participants as equal partners in knowledge production, valuing their unique perspectives. Its defining feature lies in the depth and nature of participant engagement rather than specific research methods. In participatory research, each study design is flexible and tailored through dialogue with research partners.

However, participatory research with young children is a recent development, influenced by evolving theories of childhood and the recognition of children's rights, as articulated in the UNCRC (United Nations, 1989). This shift emphasises children's right to express their own worldviews directly in research, rather than through adult proxies. In recent years, perspectives related to young children's rights have been increasingly integrated into early childhood research, an idea influenced by the New Sociology of Childhood paradigm that emphasises valuing children for who they are and acknowledging their future potential, highlighting the importance of respecting children's perspectives in research.

The concept of children as both 'beings' and 'becomings' emphasises children's right to shape both their present and future lives (Flewitt & Ang, 2020). This perspective expands on the idea of agency presented by the 'being' discourse, portraying children as active social actors who construct their everyday lives and surroundings, both presently and in the future. It encourages researchers, practitioners, and policymakers to consider children's voices in relation to their roles as agents in society. The UNCRC not only emphasises the importance of respecting children's views across various aspects of their lives but also imposes a legal obligation to do so (United Nations, 1989). Recently, children's rights to equality and empowerment have been further acknowledged in the UN 2030 agenda for sustainable development, positioning children as agents of change in societal transformation towards sustainability (United Nations, 2015). The recognition of children as active, agentic, and knowledgeable individuals has reshaped their role in research and society.

5.3 Participatory Approaches to Listening to Children's Voices

In the field of early childhood, there are several examples of approaches to pedagogy and research that are aimed at listening to young children's voices by relying on different modes of communication – verbal, non-verbal, and sensory. Indeed, the importance of listening to, and recognising young children's multiple voices, in research on matters that are relevant to them is recognised in the educational practice of the Reggio Emilia Approach to early childhood education (Rinaldi, 2021) and in the Mosaic Approach (Clark & Moss, 2011).

As an innovative approach to involving young children in research, the Reggio Emilia Approach is an example of how researchers can listen and speak to children in research by employing a variety of methods that enable children to express their views freely in multiple ways – verbally and non-verbally. Specifically, the idea of the *Hundred Languages of Children* (Edwards et al., 2011), as proposed by the Reggio Emilia Approach, points out the numerous ways children can communicate their perspectives to others, some-times without engaging in verbal communication. In Reggio Emilia settings, documentation plays a crucial role in the educational approach. It involves observing, interpreting, and reflecting on children's learning experiences to better understand their development and interests (Dahlberg et al., 2013). This process is integral to the Reggio Emilia philosophy as it helps educators tailor learning experiences to meet the unique needs of each child. Documentation in Reggio Emilia settings encompasses various forms, including written narra-tives, visual documentation such as photographs, videos, and children's art-work, oral storytelling, collaborative dialogue, and other artefacts that capture children's interactions, expressions, and learning journeys (Dahlberg et al., 2013).

Another innovative approach designed within the philosophical perspective of listening to children's voices is the Mosaic Approach, which is designed as a set of methods to gather and reflect upon the perspectives and experiences of young children (aged three to five years) in early childhood settings (Clark, 2005; Clark & Moss, 2011). The Mosaic Approach is a qualitative and multi-method partici-patory approach to data collection that enables participants (adults and children) to share their perspectives and experiences through multiple languages (Clark & Moss, 2011). The Mosaic Approach is particularly prominent in early childhood education research. It advocates for the integration of various qualitative research methods, including observations, child interviewing/conferencing, photography, book making, map making, interviews with different participants (e.g., parents and teachers), magic carpet guided tours by children, artefact sharing, and dialogical encounters, to create a comprehensive 'mosaic' of understanding (Clark & Moss, 2011).

Like the Reggio Emilia Approach to early childhood education, the Mosaic Approach acknowledges adults and children as co-constructors of meaning. Such meaning is created via verbal as well as visual means, thus offering a deeper understanding of the participants' lived experiences in one or more settings. The Reggio Emilia Approach and the Mosaic Approach are participa-tory approaches in that they view all participants as experts and active agents in their own lives; therefore, participants are involved in the decision-making process of the type of data that would be most important to share their experi-ences. Both approaches are also reflexive as they provide children with oppor-tunities to engage in multiple ways of communicating their ideas to researchers while they also contribute to the methods being employed, particularly through group dialogic encounters. Both approaches are adaptable to the participant sites and practices and do not require researchers to set up special contexts for data collection. Rather, the timing of data collection is unique to each research site. Essentially, the focus is on the participants' lived experiences, and researchers try to understand the individual experiences within a context.

The Reggio Emilia Approach and the Mosaic Approach are also embedded into early childhood practice, where the research methods used are connected to the everyday practices of the research site. Throughout the research process, researchers strive to develop a credible and collaborative relationship with participants to inform the design and development of methods to be used. More importantly, both the Reggio Emilia Approach and the Mosaic Approach respect children's agency in making decisions about their participation in research and their right to voice their opinions (Clark & Moss, 2011).

5.4 Ways of Listening to Young Children's Voices in Qualitative Research

In qualitative research, children are seen as social actors, capable of offering unique and valuable insights into their experiences and perspectives on the diverse worlds they inhabit (Flewitt & Ang, 2020). Participatory research approaches with young children are characterised by multiplicity of terms, such as 'co-production', 'co-design', and 'co-construction' (Bradbury-Jones et al., 2018, p. 81). A listening-to-children approach is tied to children's participation rights, which afford children a voice and agency in research. Consequently, the development of research that involves listening to and engaging children directly in the research process often uses creative and often child-centred research methods.

Participatory research acknowledges children's right to perspectives and ideas. In research, children can bring a fresh perspective, asking questions and contributing to knowledge in ways that adults may not consider. Therefore, participatory research methods have the potential to provide us with a snapshot into the world through the children's eyes, and make children feel heard and valued. In return, participatory research methods enhance children's sense of belonging and well-being and empower them to feel that they are listened to, and their ideas and experiences matter to the research process.

Researchers combine a range of participatory research tools to listen to children, in which levels of participation can vary (Vaughn & Jacquez, 2020). There exists a distinction drawn by some scholars between methodologies guided by adults and those led by children for the purpose of listening to children's perspectives (Urbina-Garcia et al., 2021). Adult-guided research methods include observations, structured and semi-structured interviews, group interviews, and focus groups, during which children have some degree of control but nonetheless reflect the adult interpretation of children's perspectives. Child-directed research methods include young children taking photos, drawings, draw-and-tell methods, informal discussions about children's drawings, art as a means of expressing their views, child-led tours, storytelling using props (images, cards, videos, books, or dolls), and film-based discussions. Child-directed research methods are designed to mirror the perspectives and worldviews of the children involved.

In the rest of this section, we will we will delve into various adult-guided participatory research methods available for researchers to engage with the perspectives of young children and recognise their active role in qualitative research. Following this exploration, Section 5.5 will undertake an examination of child-directed research methods.

5.4.1 Observations

Observations, a common practice in early childhood education settings, serve as valuable tools for gathering observational data in research. Observations are generally descriptive narratives of what the researchers have observed, as it happened, during any given time. In qualitative research, researchers can determine their degree of participation, ranging from complete participation, participant as observer, observer as participant, and the complete observer. In participant observations researchers try to understand what, when, where, how, and (possibly) why children act in certain ways.

During participant observations, children have a right to read field notes that concern them, and they may even ask to make amendments or add comments to the field notes (Spiteri, 2020). Comments can be written by the children, the researchers, or both. In the case of very young children, their comments and observations may be audio-recorded. Observations have the potential to bring out children's expressive competences and agency, by engaging them in the research process and by giving them a voice in research. However, researchers must determine what to observe spontaneously. Observation field notes have been criticised for being unstructured, therefore, requiring more attention at the analysis phase; are hard to compare; different interpretations are possible; and may be biased (Mukerji & Albon, 2018).

5.4.2 Journal/Diary

A novel data collection tool that is gaining interest in early childhood research is the use of a reflective journal/diary. As subjective data-gathering tools, journals or diary entries co-created by children and researchers together can increase children's participation in the research process and offer new interpretations to the data (Mukherji & Albon, 2018). Diaries and journals produced by children can be written, drawn, audio-recorded, or created using craft materials and are useful to allow children's voices to emerge and assist researchers to gain a better understanding of children's recorded thoughts and feelings in creative ways.

5.4.3 Interviews

Conversational interviews are among the most commonly used methods in early childhood research. As highly versatile research tools, interviews capture children's ideas verbally (Mukherji & Albon, 2018; Sun et al., 2023). In semi-structured or unstructured interviews, the researchers and the children engage in a conversation about an issue under study. Since young children may lack the linguistic competence to engage in conversations, researchers include a variety of creative and child-friendly data collection methods to capture children's ideas (Spiteri, 2020; Sun et al., 2023). Creative and child-friendly prompts are also used to help minimise the power imbalance between children and adult researchers, and to help children feel more comfortable expressing themselves. Even though interviews can be conducted in a variety of places, ideally, these are conducted in a place the children are familiar with, and are conducted in ways that are meaningful to children.

A number of interview techniques, such as individual or group, or a combination of both, are used when interviewing children, with conversational techniques to capture children's voices being the most commonly used. Interviews can be held in-person or online. The use of technology is not new, and digital technologies in research have been used for a long time (Fanghorban et al., 2014; Thunberg & Arnell, 2022). During the COVID-19 pandemic, online interviews using computer software that allows both audio and visual communication became useful alternatives to in-person interviews (Thunberg & Arnell, 2022). Online interviews may overcome some of the limitations presented by in-person interviews, such as financial and time constraints, as well as limitations posed by geographical and physical boundaries presented by in-person interviews (Fanghorban et al., 2014; Thunberg & Arnell, 2022). Online interviews can help increase access to participants too. In fact, online interviews proved to be beneficial for discussing several sensitive topics, such as victimisation, health issues, and sexuality, producing richer data in view of the fact that participants felt more comfortable discussing the issues, thus providing more authentic responses (Fanghorban et al., 2014; Thunberg & Arnell, 2022). Online interviews using a web camera are comparable to in-person interviews in terms of interactions between researchers and participants (Fanghorban et al., 2014). However, digital cameras can only capture a portion of the upper body of participants, thus restricting visual cues, turn-taking and participant validation, making it difficult for researchers to read visual cues and body language (Fanghorban et al., 2014; Thunberg & Arnell, 2022). Environmental factors, such as background noise, can also impact the quality of the interviews.

Participant recruitment for online and in-person interviews shares a number of similarities, including the ways participants are recruited. Informed consent and assent can be obtained online via email or posted forms, in which participants are made fully aware of the audio and/or video recordings. Obtaining online consent and maintaining anonymity were also problematic during digital interviews. Digital interviews pose ethical dilemmas nonetheless. For example, even though participants might choose to keep their cameras off, their IP address might still be tracked. Moreover, verbal and non-verbal cues can provide similar authenticity levels in both online and in-person interviews (Fanghorban et al., 2014). Additionally, when participating in online interviews, participants require high-speed internet access, familiarity with online communication, and digital literacy, all of which could affect their interactions with researchers and the way the interview is conducted (Fanghorban et al., 2014; Thunberg & Arnell, 2022).

5.4.4 Focus Groups

Focus group interview is another interview technique used in early childhood research, where children are interviewed in groups rather than individually by one or more researchers. Usually, focus groups consist of between six and twelve participants. However, in research with young children, it is reasonable to have between four and six participants in each focus group. Having a smaller number of child participants provides children with enough time and opportunities to voice their opinions. Since focus groups require interpersonal skills and can be challenging to manage, having a smaller number of children in focus groups makes it easier for the interviewer to moderate the group (Mukherji & Albon, 2018).

5.5 Visual and Arts-based Techniques

Lately, many educational researchers have directed their attention to topics within early childhood education, employing a child-centred methodology in their research endeavours. A notable emphasis has been placed on utilising visual arts as potent research instruments to actively engage young children in the research process, frequently integrating play as a mode of involvement. Such tools often intersect with creative, arts-based, game-based, and audio-visual research methodologies to facilitate dialogic co-enquiry with child participants (Ellingson & Sotirin, 2020). Arts-based techniques enable children to express ideas, thoughts, and feelings in a playful setting, there-fore, eliminating the need for the use of language. This is particularly important for young children who have not mastered the necessary language skills yet to enable them to voice their perspectives and experiences in ways that are meaningful to them and that do not necessarily rely on verbal competencies (Koller & Murphy, 2022). Additionally, arts-based techniques are useful to acknowledge children's voices when the language used is uncomfortable to express, and such data can be open to multiple interpret-ations (Ellingson & Sotirin, 2020). Such techniques also help shift the power imbalance between children and researchers, encourage dialogues between researchers and children in a way that are fun, and promote children's participation, agency, and competencies (Coyne et al., 2021). Using a range of arts-based techniques can help researchers understand the diver-sity in communication adopted by children, particularly children under age eight who may have limited language abilities (Clark, 2010). A variety of the arts-based tools commonly used in early childhood education research are discussed next.

5.5.1 Play and Toys

Usually, children embrace play and toys as these enhance their imagination. Children can engage in a variety of play as part of the research process, including role-play and imaginary play, which are often employed while they are being observed by the researchers. Researchers can also participate in children's play as part of an interview. When children and researchers play together, the adult–child power relations could dissipate, especially if they engage in non-hierarchical play, thus empowering children and enabling them to have a voice in research (Mukherji & Albon, 2018).

Early anthropological studies suggest that dolls are a common characteristic of children's play worldwide (Schwartzman, 1976). Dolls are familiar with young children and have been popular as play items for a very long time, and have been used as play items in early childhood research to elicit children's voices in a range of topics and settings (Clarke et al., 2019; Dockett et al., 2011; Johnson et al., 2014). Perhaps, their human-like appearance makes dolls a play item that children can easily engage with even during the research process, making dolls culturally relevant (Ebrahim & Francis, 2008). In fact, strong evidence suggests that dolls have been identified as effective research tools in early childhood research when they are relevant to the children's preferences, maturity level and the children's prior knowledge (Koller & Murphy, 2022). Dolls thereby allow children to openly communicate with researchers in a safe manner by overcoming difficulties associated with verbal skills (Johnson et al., 2014; Koller & Murphy, 2022). Acting as concrete, play-based, visual, and participatory tools, dolls are used by researchers as an effective method for exercising children's rights to a voice while exploring their perspectives in a variety of studies and across a range of topics, giving a voice to children, particularly those whose perspectives are overlooked (Koller & Murphy, 2022). In research, dolls have been used as part of a story completion for data collection purposes (Clarke et al., 2019; Ebrahim & Francis, 2008).

5.5.2 Stories

Stories as research techniques were first used in developmental psychology and psychotherapy as projective tools in clinical assessments and also in quantitative research (Moller et al., 2021). Nowadays, stories created by children are used to help researchers explore the meanings children ascribe to a particular topic of interest (Lenette et al., 2022; Moller et al., 2021). Children's stories are useful because they provide children with multiple opportunities to talk about their experiences (Clarke et al., 2019; Ebrabim & Francis, 2008; Lenette et al., 2022).

Story compilation is another storytelling technique used in both qualitative and quantitative early childhood research. As a qualitative data collection technique, story completion was originally developed within the field of psychoanalysis as a projective technique or to be used as a clinical assessment tool in developmental psychology research to assess attachment, as well as in consumer and feminist research (see Clarke et al., 2019). Story completion requires children to write a story by first being given a cue (a hypothetical scenario created by the researchers) and a set of instructions to follow in order to complete the story (Clarke et al., 2019). The uptake of story completion as a research method in early childhood has been minimal until recently; however, the emancipatory potential of stories as research methods across diverse research areas is growing (Nur & Arnas, 2022). Nevertheless, 'story completion cannot capture the complexity of the social world – no method can completely' (Clarke et al., 2019, p. 16), but it can serve as a comprehensive and developmentally appropriate way of asserting children's agency while exploring their ideas through their narratives.

5.5.3 Photographs and Videos

Many children like to play with dolls or take part in role-plays in research. Yet children may prefer other research tools, such as cameras, over dolls (Dockett et al., 2011). In fact, photo-elicitation is another technique used by researchers to gain young children's visual representation of an issue. Photographs provided by the children have been used as child-friendly visual methods by several early childhood researchers to elicit young children's ideas about the issue under study during interviews. Children's photographs provide different information that may be missed during verbal interviews alone. Children's photographs can also be used to act as an icebreaker or as a focus for further discussion during an interview. Photographs are also useful tools to disseminate information and talk about issues that would be otherwise difficult to tackle with young children. In this way, children's photographs are viewed as a means for children to assert their voices and agency in the research process because children can choose what is to be photographed and what is not to be photographed, and they can choose how and when to talk about their photographs during research. Due to their artistic and metaphorical potential, and their potential to generate reflective thoughts, photographs can introduce new aesthetic dimensions in the way children process knowledge in aesthetically and communicatively efficient ways. As visual data, photographs may present different perspectives other than those of the researchers. Therefore, it is recommended that children are interviewed about their photographs. During interviews, researchers can follow up on, or revisit, ideas that are captured on a photograph at a later date, making photographs an ideal tool for generating data in case studies with young children.

Like photographs, videos can be produced by children to voice their perspectives in research. Videos have the potential to involve young children directly in the documentation process of a research project while bypassing the written word (Blaisdell et al., 2022). To date, little research has focused on the use of digital video technologies in early childhood research to explore young children's experiences and thought processes (Elwick, 2015; Flewitt, 2022). Whenever videos have been used in early childhood research, these were used to record observations (Elwick, 2015). More research exploring the use of children's videos as qualitative research tools is warranted.

5.5.4 Drawings

Art is closely related to children's thinking because children's drawings are believed to closely represent their worldviews (Vygotsky, 1971). Children's drawings in research acknowledge their agency, and allow children the freedom to express their ideas in an unguided manner. Children's drawings can act as icebreakers and provide researchers with opportunities to build a rapport with children as research participants. Since children's drawings provide visual data, children's interpretations of their own drawings during an interview are also used as data collection tools in childhood research (Clark & Moss, 2011; Spiteri, 2020). Children's interpretations of their own drawings generated via interviews serve a dual role. First, they minimise the chances of imposing an adult-centric interpretation to children's drawings; and second, they allow children to express their ideas about what matters to them; hence, they assert their voices in research. Therefore, in order to obtain an adequate interpretation of children's drawings in ways that are true to children's voices, it is crucial to involve children in clarifying meanings embedded in their creative outputs (Dockett et al., 2009).

5.6 The Challenges of Research Participation by Young Children

Even though creative and participatory research methods are used to encourage young children to participate in the research process, it is essential to recognise the challenges associated with these approaches. For a start, participatory techniques with young children are not a quick way of collecting data with young children. Rather such techniques require careful planning and preparation, and are time-consuming. Researchers are advised to engage in a critical evaluation and reflection process concerning the utilisation of participatory research methods with children, with the objective of comprehensively examining both the benefits and drawbacks associated with such approaches (Punch, 2002).

Children's participation challenges the dominant discourse around children's vulnerability, dependence, and development, and eliminates many of the power structures present between children and adults (Tisdall, 2015). Yet conducting research with children presents notable practical and methodological hurdles, which advocates of participatory research may sometimes overlook (Flewitt & Ang, 2020). The process has been described by some as 'Pollyanna-ish', suggesting that participatory approaches still fail to challenge the very power relations they aim to disrupt (Blaisdell et al., 2022). The question remains as to which participatory, age-appropriate, and child-friendly research methods can be used when conducting research with young children. The widespread misinterpretation regarding children's involvement in research arises from researchers frequently claiming to conduct participatory research, yet resorting to tokenistic practices instead (Morrow, 2008). Tokenism results in children's involvement being passive rather than active. Over time, efforts have been made to distinguish between tokenistic participation and genuinely empowering roles for children in research.

Participatory research calls for children to be involved in the research process right from the beginning, as enshrined in the UNCRC (United Nations, 1989).

Yet, in reality, this decision-making process remains a challenge to implement. In research with young children, careful attention to the design of the research methods is required, ensuring that potential threats to children are eliminated. More than this, the complexity involved in the child-researcher relationship has increased the focus on adopting participatory methods in research involving children. Hence, young children's ability to participate in, and contribute towards, the research process is not to be underestimated.

Researchers bear the responsibility of devising research methodologies conducive to meaningful engagement by children. The 'ladder of children's participation' (Hart, 1992) delineates eight levels of involvement, with each level describing different levels of children's involvement and empowerment in the research process. The initial three levels are characterised as non-participation (manipulation, decoration and tokenism), while subsequent levels denote increasing degrees of engagement, spanning from assigned but informed roles to shared decision-making initiated by the child alongside adults. Many researchers employ Hart's framework to evaluate the authenticity of children's involvement in participatory research, acknowledging the limitations associated with lower levels of engagement. Nevertheless, criticism has been levied against Hart's ladder for its hierarchical structure, which may imply that full participation holds superiority over other forms of engagement, despite the potential challenges in achieving or appropriateness of full participation in all contexts.

An alternative model consisting of five stages is presented by Shier (2001), emphasising the dedication of adults to empowering children, with each stage including specific objectives aimed at assessing the level of child participation. Shier's participation model includes stages where children are involved in decision-making processes, and share power and responsibility for decision-making. Similar to Hart's (1992) model, Shier's (2001) framework has been both praised and criticised. Some appreciate its utility in guiding participatory research design, while others critique its failure to acknowledge the dynamic nature of power negotiation in research decision-making (Flewitt & Ang, 2020). Additionally, Shier's model has been criticised for focusing on what happens to children in research rather than emphasising their active role and status, and for lacking adequate theorisation of children's participation (Flewitt & Ang, 2020). To support the design of participatory research, Stephenson (2009) developed a set of 'checking questions' aimed at prioritising children's perspectives. These questions encompass considerations such as initiating with children's thoughts, integrating their ideas throughout each stage, refraining from suggestive questioning, and remaining receptive to following the children's direction. Despite their shortcomings, together, these models can help researchers consider the varying degrees of children's participation in the research process based on the research aims and context, preventing participation from becoming overly prescriptive or restrictive.

The defining feature of participatory research is recognising children as experts in their own lives, empowering them to express their views in their preferred manner, and prioritising their perspectives. This shift in approach requires a fundamental re-evaluation of relationships within the research process, and challenges the traditional roles of academic researchers and child participants in participatory research. Researchers dedicated to promoting children's full participation in research have the responsibility not only to involve children in disseminating research findings but also to engage them in deciding the impact of their work (Flewitt & Ang, 2020). However, it is observed that children are not consistently included in research write-ups and impact events. During the early planning and research design phases, researchers can use research questions and models to consider the varying degrees of children's participation (Flewitt & Ang, 2020). This spectrum ranges from children taking the leading role in all research stages, to children informing the research designed that is conducted by adults. Even though most participatory research falls between these two extremes, the choice of participation depends on the research objectives. Therefore, it is important that researchers ensure that whenever young children are involved as researchers in participatory research, they understand the realistic potential impact of their work to prevent feelings of neglect or dismissal.

Even if researchers follow ethical guidelines carefully, their research methods can still be problematic. In relation to knowing what to research and with whom, the researchers' effects are possible. Conducting research with young children requires training, skill, and practice. Typically, participatory research involves mentorship, where experienced researchers train new researchers in data collection techniques and ethics, enabling new participants to experiment with and discuss various approaches. At every stage of the research process, researchers also need to keep in mind how their presence may be influencing children's responses and the type of communication that happens when children and researchers engage in dialogues. During this process, researchers can learn about participants' interests and communication styles.

Conducting research with children involves communication. Participatory research requires researchers to build a rapport with the children. As a result, a relationship between the adult researchers and the child participant is often developed. In early childhood research, attention is given to how children convey thoughts, views, and intentions through language, actions, and social interactions. In this relationship, dialogue plays a key role in helping researchers understand the child's point of view. By understanding children's communication styles, researchers can engage in meaningful dialogue, fostering trust and developing innovative research methods that align with children's perspectives. However, language competence and cognitive overload can make dialogues challenging and may create a power imbalance between the adult researchers and child participants, and these can impact the authenticity of any communication between the two (Spiteri, 2020). Consequently, researchers need to be mindful of their critical role when conducting qualitative research with young children. For research with young children to be ethical, researchers need to have a good understanding of what a researcher is and what its role is. Therefore, it is worth considering the role of the researcher and the relationships of power that emerge during the research process. The first imbalance in the relationship is created by the fact that the researcher is an adult. Since children are in the least powerful position in the research (Barratt Hacking et al., 2013), the presence of an adult researcher, or possibly more than one researcher, puts children in a subordinate position and could potentially also make them vulnerable to abuse (Gallagher, 2009). Issues of power could easily subordinate children (MacNaughton, 2005) in the sense that some children may believe that they are expected to fully participate in the research process because subordination has always been demanded from the adults around them (Aubrey & Dahl, 2005). Although power relations cannot be totally eliminated, children's welfare should always be prioritised by researchers during the entire research process. Lastly, if academic research is to be published, such intentions are to be communicated and explained honestly and responsibly to the participants before the research process begins (Gilliat-Ray et al., 2022).

5.7 Critiques of Qualitative Research

Despite its goals towards children's full and meaningful participation in research, qualitative research has faced its fair share of criticism. Critiques of qualitative research in early childhood encompass a broad spectrum of perspectives and considerations that are continuously evolving (Scott & Usher, 2011). Indeed, scholars are actively engaged in ongoing critical dialogue aimed at refining methodological approaches and addressing inherent limitations (Cohen et al., 2018).

Qualitative research has been criticised for being anecdotal or illustrative, and that it is practised in casual and unsystematic ways (Mason, 2018). Such critique is based on a misunderstanding of the logic of qualitative enquiry, and fails to see the strategic significance of context and the development of our understandings and explanations of the social world (Mason, 2018). Given its focus on the in-depth exploration within specific contexts, qualitative research has also been criticised for its lack of generalisability and transferability of findings to broader populations or settings, limiting the applicability of the findings (Stake, 2006). Qualitative research conceptualises generalisability in a distinct manner compared to quantitative research. Quantitative research employs a large random sample that mirrors the broader population to minimise individual differences and facilitate statistical inference applicable to the entire population. In contrast, qualitative research prioritises obtaining individual insights rather than striving for a representative sample. Top of Form Qualitative research seldom relies on random sampling, making it unsuitable for making references to broader populations as done in surveys conducted for quantitative analysis.

Since qualitative research prioritises depth and richness of data, traditional criteria for validity and reliability may be perceived as less applicable. As a result, critics argue that ensuring the trustworthiness of qualitative findings can be challenging, particularly regarding issues of credibility, transferability, dependability, and confirmability (Guba & Lincoln, 2018). To overcome these challenges, researchers need to employ rigorous methods to enhance the trustworthiness of their work (Guba & Lincoln, 2018; Stake, 2006).

Another key concern regarding qualitative research is its vulnerability to researcher bias and subjectivity. Reflexivity serves as a response to this critique (Cohen et al., 2018; Mason, 2018). Through a critical reflexive approach, qualitative researchers actively acknowledge and address their own subjectivity and potential biases throughout the research process, enhancing the credibility and trustworthiness of qualitative findings by minimising the impact of researcher bias (Mason, 2018; Stake, 2006).

Qualitative research frequently involves close and prolonged interaction with participants that may uncover sensitive or personal information about young children. In early childhood research, it is crucial to uphold ethical standards, including ensuring informed consent from adults, assent from children, the protection of privacy and confidentiality, and the management of power dynamics between researchers and participants (Lundy, 2007). This highlights the necessity for researchers to engage in ethical reflexivity and adhere closely to established guidelines to uphold the rights and well-being of all participants, particularly young children (Ellingson & Sotirin, 2020; Gallagher, 2009).

Employing participatory research methods that empower young children as active participants in the research process may offer a pathway to addressing entrenched power imbalances in early childhood research. However, participatory research methods have been criticised for falling short of achieving the objectives of qualitative research to effect change, underestimating power imbalances between researchers and child participants, lacking clear methods of data collection and analysis, and being under-theorised. Concerns also exist regarding the impact of participatory research methods on children's lives and the underrepresentation of certain groups, such as children with disabilities. Critics point out the paradox that initiating participatory research often requires researchers from privileged, educated backgrounds, raising questions about its democratic nature (Bergold & Thomas, 2012). Another common criticism of participatory research methods is that not all children may enjoy or find it easy to engage with the research process (Spiteri, 2020). Participatory research methods are still marked by uncertainty and the recognition that the effectiveness of research methods depends on how such methods are applied and the effectiveness of the attitudes guiding their use. Therefore, a key aspect of participatory research involves understanding children's communication styles, fostering dialogue, and building trust with them, which can also positively impact relationships between children and caregivers in their communities. Remaining open, flexible, and responsive to children's perspectives throughout the research process is essential for its success.

The intricate nature of qualitative data analysis can pose challenges concerning transparency, reliability, and validity in analysis, especially in large-scale studies. To mitigate these concerns, researchers need to adopt transparent and systematic methodologies for coding, categorising, and interpreting qualitative data, to ensure reliability, transparency, rigour, and trustworthiness (Cresswell & Poth, 2018).

While these critiques raise important considerations for qualitative researchers, they also underscore the ongoing efforts within the field to address methodological challenges, enhance rigour, and advance ethical practice. By engaging in reflexive inquiry, methodological innovation, and interdisciplinary collaboration, qualitative researchers can continue to strengthen the credibility and impact of their work.

5.8 Concluding Comments

Participatory research with children is still evolving. This section has shown the wide range of methods, from dialogic approaches to full involvement of children in all research stages that encompass participatory research. Despite this diversity, participatory methods share the common goal of amplifying children's voices and empowering children to voice their opinion and assert their agency in research. Participatory research is a democratic, empowering, and ethical way of conducting early childhood research. Here, children are often considered as co-researchers during part of, or the entire, research process. As the field progresses, there's a need for deeper reflection and alignment between theory, methodology, and research methods, with ongoing scrutiny of the concept of 'children's voices and agency'. Despite the challenge of fully understanding children's perspectives, participatory research enables researchers to demonstrate their competences and address the prevailing power imbalances between adults and children in both research and broader society.

6 Mixed Methods Research in Early Childhood

Section 6 delves into mixed methods design, which incorporates both quantitative and qualitative research methods. At first glance, this section looks like it provides a combination of the research methods discussed in the previous sections. Even though at times this may be the case, there are several methodological distinctions that will be noted here.

This section explores the distinct methodologies associated with each approach, highlighting the diverse insights they offer into early childhood research and their varying impacts on educational change. It provides examples of mixed methods studies, ranging from small- to large-scale, demonstrating how mixed methods approaches contribute to a more comprehensive understanding of a variety of themes and contexts in early childhood research.

6.1 The Qualitative and Quantitative Divide

Historically, qualitative and quantitative methods were perceived as conflicting paradigms. Throughout the 1980s and 1990s, debates between proponents of experimental and interpretive methodologies led to a paradigmatic divide, with qualitative methods gaining legitimacy for studying complex social phenomena. However, in recent decades there has been a shift towards bridging the gap between the two paradigms, collaboration between experimental and interpretive research, recognising the complementary insights each approach offers, leading to the emergence of mixed methods research as a distinct methodology (Flewitt & Ang, 2020).

Over time, mixed methods research design has gained popularity, particularly in the social sciences like education and sociology (Pearce, 2012). The term 'mixed methods' encompasses the integration of both quantitative and qualitative methods, or data within a single study or design. Quantitative research addresses questions of 'what', 'where', 'when', and 'how much', whereas qualitative research delves into 'why' and 'how' questions. By combining both quantitative and qualitative approaches, researchers can design studies that provide comprehensive insights into educational experiences and opportunities for young children, leveraging the strengths of each methodology.

Various definitions highlight this integration, emphasising the collection, analysis, and integration of data from both approaches. In mixed methods research, researchers collect and analyse data, integrate findings, and draw inferences using both quantitative and qualitative approaches in a single study (Cohen et al., 2018; Corr et al., 2020; Mertens, 2015; Tashakkori & Creswell, 2007). Mixed methods research is described as 'better suited to developing theoretical and practical models of information behaviour … [they] are vital to allow deeper insights to emerge by placing methods in conversation with each other' (Gooding, 2021, p. 146). Broadly speaking, mixed methods research can capture a diverse range of perspectives not possible in traditional quantitative or qualitative methods alone (Cohen et al., 2018; Flewitt & Ang, 2020; Mertens, 2015). By combining quantitative and qualitative methods, researchers can obtain a richer perspective, ultimately enhancing our knowledge of early childhood education and informing educational practices on a broader scale.

Mixed methods research has evolved into a distinct methodology with its own worldview and techniques, providing researchers with a comprehensive approach to investigating complex phenomena and yielding new discoveries and understandings. In recent years, mixed methods research has expanded into various fields, including health and medical sciences, nursing, family medicine, mental health, pharmacy, and other related life sciences disciplines (Flewitt & Ang, 2020). Over the past thirty years, numerous authors have highlighted the versatility, applicability, and utility of using a mixed methods approach to early childhood research too (Corr et al., 2020; Flewitt & Ang, 2020; Gooding, 2021; Liebenberg & Ungar, 2015). Mixed methods research offers opportunities for generating new research questions, designs, and insights, ultimately contributing to enhanced research rigour and validity.

Mixed methods research has been called the 'third methodological movement' (Teddlie & Tashakkori, 2009). Some critics argue that mixed methods research can become overly focused on methodology at the expense of theory; however, proponents emphasise its capacity to capture complexity and diversity within a subject area (Flewitt & Ang, 2020). As a paradigm, mixed methods research asserts that the research does not necessarily need to be conducted exclusively via quantitative or qualitative research, but rather a mixture of both (Cohen et al., 2018). With theoretical roots in pragmatism, claims made from mixed methods research go beyond the data types to include its own paradigm, ontology, epistemology, axiology, and methodologies which inform the design and conduct of research studies (Cohen et al., 2018). However, some argue that pragmatists consider the research questions to be the most important factor for determining the choice of methodology, rejecting the postpositivist and the constructive paradigms (Teddlie & Tashakkori, 2009). Despite such debates, the central premise of mixed methods research is that the collection, analyses, and mixing of both quantitative and qualitative data in one study or in a series of studies provide a better understanding of the research problem than single methods approach, and answer complex research questions with generality, thus providing richer and more robust studies compared to single method approaches (Cohen et al., 2018).

6.2 Mixed Methods in Early Childhood Research

In early childhood research, mixed methods can be particularly valuable in trying to solve complex social questions that could not be answered in any other way (Mertens, 2015); however, doing so necessitates meticulous research design (Flewitt & Ang, 2020). Like in other sectors of educational research, in early childhood research, a mixed methods approach bridges the divide between qualitative and quantitative research, in which diverse approaches, designs, and interpretations are integrated (Flewitt & Ang, 2020). Such integration involves creatively sequencing and implementing qualitative and quantitative methods across different phases or strands of the research. However, this bridge metaphor is not a true representation of the full range of possibilities that mixed methods approach can offer to early childhood research (Corr et al., 2020). In a mixed methods approach, researchers mix methods, methodologies, theories, standpoints, and paradigm assumptions from qualitative and quantitative approaches (Corr et al., 2020). From this perspective, as a methodological approach, mixed methods offer new ways of cultivating new and creative ways of thinking and new ways of researching an issue, possibly leading to unexpected findings (Flewitt & Ang, 2020).

As a methodological approach, mixed methods are increasingly used in early childhood research, including early childhood special education research (Corr et al., 2020). In the literature, mixed methods research has been effectively utilised for exploring programme outcomes, investigating research questions, and evaluating large-scale research projects (Doyle et al., 2022). The suitability of a mixed methods approach to capturing young children's voices and agency in early childhood research depends on several factors, including the phenomenon under investigation, the research questions, the sociocultural context in which the study is conducted, and the funding agency's requirements. Since mixed methods research can refer to the use of both quantitative and qualitative methods to answer the research questions in one study, the researchers need to either be experts in both, or to employ a group of experts to assist with the study design and analysis of the data (Cohen et al., 2018; Mertens, 2015).

6.3 Mixed Methods Research as a Way of Listening to Young Children's Voices

Mixed methods design can fit within a transformative framework, making the design suitable for advocacy purposes (Mertens, 2009, 2015). As a framework, a mixed methods design aligns well with the advocacy for children's rights as promoted by the UNCRC (United Nations, 1989). More broadly, in early childhood education research, mixed methods approaches have been popular and useful in providing opportunities for listening to children.

The Reggio Emilia Approach (Rinaldi, 2021) and the Mosaic Approach (Clark & Moss, 2011) (see Section 5.3) adopt mixed methods approach to generating data with children, making these approaches transformative in nature by empowering children to express their ideas about their experiences, using verbal and non-verbal communication. Multiple ways of listening offer an opportunity for adults and children to listen to each other and to reflect on each other's worldviews (Rinaldi, 2021). Similarly, mixed methods research adopts multiple data collection methods to listen to children's voices, which requires adults to relearn other ways that would enable them to communicate with young children (Clark, 2005; Edwards et al., 2011). In this regard, multiple ways of listening place emphasis on listening as an ethical issue (Clark, 2005). Taken together, the Reggio Emilia Approach and the Mosaic Approach provide support for the benefits of using mixed methods designs in early childhood research in order to listen to young children and acknowledge their agency. Furthermore, the different methods adopted in these two approaches enable researchers to gain different understandings of the different dimensions of listening to children. From this perspective, mixed methods research offers a powerful case for listening to young children's voices.

Developed in the context of early childhood research, multi-method approaches to listening to children recognise the different voices of young children and adults (parents and educators), acknowledging the contributions each could make to the research process (Clark & Moss, 2011). Using diverse methods to make children's voices visible, such as observations, interviews, photography, and book making, a mixed methods approach brings together a range of qualitative and quantitative methods to listen to children's ideas about their lives (Clark, 2005). By adopting a mixed methods design, data are collected via a combination of techniques to create a multifaceted framework that facilitates the process of listening to young children's voices.

Even though strong evidence suggests the utility of a mixed methods approach in effectively exploring young children's voices about their lives in the early years, there remains little evidence of methodological innovation within the field to make mixed methods research more mainstream (Corr et al., 2020; Flewitt & Ang, 2020; Liebenberg & Ungar, 2015). Perhaps this is because a mixed methods design requires careful planning of how the diverse methods can work together in synergy (Cohen et al., 2018).

6.4 Designing Mixed Methods Research

The design of mixed methods research uses techniques from qualitative and quantitative research traditions, simultaneously or sequentially (Mertens, 2015). Four approaches to mixed methods research design are commonly adopted in early childhood research (Cohen et al., 2018; Flewitt & Ang, 2020). The first three designs follow a sequential pattern of investigation; the fourth design occurs concurrently and is integrated in both qualitative and quantitative methods.

Qualitative-Quantitative Sequential Exploration: Involves a sequential approach, where qualitative exploration precedes a larger quantitative survey, using identified themes from the qualitative phase as a foundation for quantitative analysis. In a mixed methods study about food safety knowledge in Hispanic families with young children, Stenger et al. (2014) began their study with a qualitative inquiry using focus groups, followed by a quantitative survey. Similarly, qualitative methods can be utilised by researchers to gain access to young children's specific knowledge about patterning skills in order to develop theoretical concepts; these findings can then be used to inform the quantitative sub-study (Luken & Sauzet, 2021). Here, the quantitative methods can be used to provide the researchers with an overview of the domain under study and describe its heterogeneity.

Questionnaire-Driven Qualitative Exploration: Also sequential, beginning with a questionnaire to uncover issues, followed by qualitative exploration of identified topics with a purposively chosen sample. A mixed methods approach can be employed to explore young children's participation in diverse educational settings, utilising a demographic questionnaire followed by a narrative data collection strategy (Benjamin et al., 2017). Similarly, in a mixed methods investigation, the researchers can begin with a questionnaire to explore the effects of education provision on preschool children's attainment, social, and behavioural development upon school entry and even later, followed by observational data and interviews with in-depth case studies (Sammons et al., 2005).

Multi-Phase Sequential Mixed Methods Analysis: Utilises a sequential pattern with multiple phases, alternating between questionnaire, qualitative exploration, and experimental testing, aimed at building a conceptual understanding and conducting statistical analysis. In a large cohort mixed methods study, the researchers initiated their study with a large questionnaire, followed by an in-depth qualitative investigation and finishing their study with a statistical analysis about novel situations such as the COVID-19 pandemic (Nguyen et al., 2023).

Concurrent Mixed Methods Inquiry: Employs concurrent quantitative and qualitative methods within a single study, allowing for demographic analysis, statistical assessment of ratings responses, and qualitative coding of open-ended questions, facilitating comprehensive data interpretation. In their study about risky play in early childhood, LeMasters and Vandermaas-Peeler (2023) initiated their study by conducting a survey that concluded with five open-ended questions, followed by observations, focus groups and semi-structured interviews. In an iterative mixed methods study, Liebenberg and Ungar (2015) worked with marginalised populations initiating the study with a quantitative approach and simultaneously integrated a qualitative design to collect relevant data simultaneously. Here, children were involved as co-researchers, where a photo-elicitation approach to data collection was used, thus demonstrating that young children are capable of participating in various stages of a mixed methods study design and data analysis. The researchers conclude that they were able to ensure internal validity and generalisability of the resilience construct, and improve the research design.

Together, these studies showcase the versatility of mixed methods research and highlight the importance of tailoring designs to research questions and aims. Careful consideration of mixed methods dimensions allows for new theoretical and paradigmatic reflections, offering researchers opportunities for comprehensive investigation and insight generation (Flewitt & Ang, 2020).

6.5 Triangulation, Reliability, and Validity

Mixed methods research can help address concerns related to the internal validity and generalisability currently present in early childhood research, across cultures. Combining quantitative and qualitative data collection methods offers greater opportunities for triangulation and may strengthen the validity, reliability, dependability, credibility, and accuracy of the findings (Cohen et al., 2018). Different data sources are validated via different methods, which in turn provide multiple perspectives, improving the validity and reliability of the findings and conclusions (Liebenberg & Ungar, 2015).

Triangulation of the data, or the validation of research findings by comparing different data sources, is at the core of a mixed methods research design (Flewitt & Ang, 2020; Gooding, 2021; Luken & Suazet, 2021). Triangulation involves corroborating findings from qualitative and quantitative data to assess the credibility of inferences. Beyond methods, respondent validation, engaging with participants' perspectives, is crucial for ensuring validity across research approaches. Since mixed methods research integrates multiple research methods, triangulation promises greater rigour of the study design and the research process (Liebenberg & Ungar, 2015). Through triangulation of the data from multiple methods or lenses simultaneously, alternative perspectives could be obtained because findings from quantitative data can be compared with findings from quantitative data (Mertens, 2015).

In mixed methods research, quantitative and qualitative techniques are seen as complementary perspectives, seeking to answer the research questions in intuitive and expansive ways, while meeting the needs of multiple audiences for results. However, Cohen et al. (2018) argue that the claim of mixed methods research being complementary is not justifiable in that it is up to the researchers to decide whether a method is complementary or whether it supplements the study. When deciding whether to choose a mixed methods approach, researchers should assess whether the method itself can adequately address the research questions independently, rather than emphasising how the methods might mutually enhance each other (complementary) or provide additional support or insights (supplementary). Ultimately, a strong mixed methods study asks what could be gained and/or lost by using mixed methods research; how the method deals with the objectivity and the subjectivity of the study; and how would the study turn out by not using mixed methods research.

6.6 Critiques of Mixed Methods

Mixed methods research has gained traction in early childhood educational research due to its ability to provide a comprehensive understanding of complex social phenomena (Flewitt & Ang, 2020). Indeed, many researchers acknowledge the benefits of mixed methods research in effectively managing the interplay between qualitative and quantitative methods (Flewitt & Ang, 2020). Yet mixed methods research is not the answer for every research project (Cohen et al., 2018; Creswell & Plano Clark, 2018). The process and degree of integration, known as mixing and assimilation of data, present major challenges. In fact, the recent developments in mixed methods research have generated an array of insightful critiques regarding the theoretical development and methodological practices of this research approach (Corr et al., 2020; Fàbregues et al., 2021).

Most criticism in the field is related to the definition of mixed methods, as well as its philosophy, procedures, and politics (Creswell & Plano Clark, 2018; Fàbregues et al., 2021). Combining quantitative and qualitative data collection and analysis in one study may be difficult as both methodologies follow different ontologies, epistemologies, methodologies, axiologies, data types, and so on (Cohen et al., 2018). Specifically, the different epistemological and philosophical frameworks guiding mixed methods research make it difficult for many researchers to ensure its suitability for the research design, as well as its robustness and reliability of the research findings (Dawadi et al., 2021). As a result, some critics question whether a mixed methods approach is even a paradigm, and numerous questions remain unanswered (Cohen et al., 2018).

Mixed methods research aims to produce an outcome that surpasses the mere combination of qualitative and quantitative components. Yet the feasibility of integrating qualitative and quantitative methods is questioned due to the conflicting nature of data generated from incompatible methods (Flewitt & Ang, 2020). Consequently, mixed methods research requires researchers to acquire the skills of both quantitative and qualitative research approaches, in addition to a solid grounding in mixed methods methodology before designing mixed methods research (Creswell & Plano Clark, 2018). Achieving this outcome requires striking a balance between the two datasets without marginalising either method.

Mixed methods research poses increasing demands on researchers because it is time-consuming and requires a variety of resources to meet the needs of both qualitative and quantitative data collection, integration, and analysis (Creswell & Plano Clark, 2018; Dawadi et al., 2021). Other challenges of mixed methods research include verifying inferences from convergent data, interpreting discrepancies, and explicitly reporting insights gained from both approaches (Corr et al., 2020; Plano Clark & Ivankova, 2016). As a result, data collection can be lengthy, and considering the amount of data generated, data analysis can be difficult to integrate (Barata & Yosikawa, 2014). In fact, there is ongoing debate about the status of qualitative research within mixed methods, with concerns that it may be relegated to a supporting role. Therefore, it's crucial for both qualitative and quantitative data to be treated with equal rigour to ensure credible inferences (Creswell & Plano Clark, 2018; Cohen et al., 2018).

The researchers' alignment with diverse communities of practice seems to influence the way the divergent methodological approaches are applied in mixed methods research (Fàbregues et al., 2021). Some scholars argue for a more extensive qualitative approach driven by a social justice agenda within mixed methods designs, emphasising the importance of diversity and transformative social justice projects (Flewitt & Ang, 2020). In mixed methods research, researchers are to recognise and explain the underlying frameworks guiding their design, data collection, analysis, and interpretation processes, thus enhancing the rigour and quality of mixed methods research (Corr et al., 2020).

6.7 Concluding Comments

This section examined mixed methods research as a way of looking at the social world of young children from different perspectives. Employing a mixed methods design demands thoughtful consideration and sophistication beyond simply combining methods. Rather, researchers need to carefully assess the appropriateness of a mixed methods approach and establish a clear purpose for their study. Important decisions regarding research questions, paradigms, and data collection methods need to be made to effectively address the research objectives.

This section also raised some challenges of the use of mixed methods in early childhood research. Understanding the variations in mixed methods research helps researchers weigh the strengths and limitations to determine if it aligns with their study's goals. When well planned and executed, mixed methods studies can contribute to generating innovative research agendas in early childhood education, and provide insights into complex social phenomena, enhancing the validity and reliability of findings, and reconciling contradictions between quantitative and qualitative results (Flewitt & Ang, 2020). Finally, a well-designed mixed methods study can uncover new knowledge in early childhood education by allowing methodologies to inform each other effectively.

7 Conclusion and Future Directions

This Element highlighted the different research methods that can be used to elicit young children's voices and agency. It has provided a discussion around a range of research methods that can support researchers in dialogue with children. Rather than simply presenting a set of simple data collection methods, this Element has demonstrated how quantitative, qualitative, and mixed methods methodologies have the capacity to impact children's meaningful participation in research, by facilitating their voices and agency. Children gain so much more from research when they are treated as meaningful participants, and even co-researchers, in the research process, rather than just sources of information. Meaningful participation allows young children to feel empowered to express their ideas and explore new and complex topics through the use of their imagination.

Throughout this Element, the importance of grounding early childhood education research in a robust theoretical framework and adapting methodologies to suit specific research goals has been emphasised. In doing so, this Element highlighted the complexity involved in conducting research with young children in ways that acknowledge their voices and agency. However, the methods discussed in here are not definitive. Rather, researchers are encouraged to use the diverse research methods discussed here in a critical manner. It is hoped that the insights and ideas presented in the Element inspire researchers to use diverse research methods that listen to children's voices and acknowledge their agency in a space that is adapted to diverse cultural contexts.

This Element has positioned young children as having a right to participate in meaningful research that concerns them. Empirical research involves actively seeking new information through observation, testimony collection, or re-examination of existing data. Overall, when approaching research from a children's rights perspective, it is clear that those with expertise in early childhood development and research, whether researchers, educators or policy-makers, face some obligation. Ethical considerations are paramount, requiring respect for the rights of all participants, including obtaining appropriate per-missions and avoiding judgement of children's lives. In early childhood research, fundamental principles of systematic, critically reflective, empirical, and ethical research must be upheld. Studies need to be meticulously designed and explained to ensure replicability, with clear articulation of aims, theoretical frameworks, research context, sample, and methods. Finally, researchers need to uphold a critical and reflective mindset, questioning their own beliefs and societal discourses.

7.1 What Next?

This Element provides the theoretical and practical tools to undertake research in early childhood. Yet there is important work ahead for early childhood researchers. Further research into understanding young children's worlds through diverse methods is still required. The diverse research methods dis-cussed in this Element could be used to explore complex issues that young children might find difficult to talk about in diverse sociocultural settings.

Further implementation of diverse research methods that are culturally sen-sitive to the children's needs offers potential opportunities to increase the impact of early childhood research and enhance young children's voices and agency in research about issues that matter to them. This is an important endeavour because unless children's voices are listened to and understood, it is unlikely that their voices will be taken seriously. When children's voices are taken seriously in policy and practice, the resultant outcome will be more socially and culturally relevant to children's lives and experiences, therefore enhancing their rights and agency more broadly.

7.2 Ethical Dissemination

The temporal aspect of children's participation in research is worth taking into consideration, especially since such a process is built on trust, and the level of influence and interdependence in the child–adult relationship. Children's participation in research presents researchers with ethical, methodological, and practical dilemmas (Bishop, 2014; Bradbury-Jones et al., 2018). In research that is still overwhelmingly interpreted and disseminated by adults, how can children's voices be equally and ethically disseminated?

The main aim of dissemination is to create change, for example, by influencing policy or teacher training programmes. Multiple modes of dissemination exist. Some modes of dissemination are more accessible to children than others. These can include online sources such as blogs, policy papers, and public presentations. It is increasingly common in educational research to include a number of stakeholders and/or participants, ranging from children, teachers, parents, professionals, researchers, and policymakers, as part of the dissemination process.

With the rise of digital media, the dissemination of research findings via video material shared online is becoming more mainstream. However, tracing the material can become almost impossible to control especially when there is a breach of participant confidentiality. Ethical dissemination of early childhood research includes (a) seeking the consent of children and their families prior to making the material public; (b) conducting a final feedback interview to help children select which data they want to share; and (c) seeking the approval of transcription and analysis of audio and visual data prior to dissemination (Johnson et al., 2014). Therefore, early childhood researchers have ethical responsibilities to share research findings in ways that protect children's anonymity while simultaneously honouring their voices. In conclusion, it is my greatest hope that these approaches will help create new research stories that will improve the field of early childhood research and put children's voices at the forefront of cutting-edge research.

References

Aubrey, C., & Dahl, S. (2005). That child needs a good listening to! Reviewing effective interview strategies. *Journal of Education, 35*, 99–119. https://doi.org/10.10520/AJA0259479X_108

Barata, M. C., & Yoshikawa, H. (2014). Mixed methods in research on child well-being. In A. Ben-Arieh, F. Casas, I. Frønes, & J. Korbin (Eds.). *Handbook of child well-being* (pp. 2879–2893). Springer. https://doi.org/10.1007/978-90-481-9063-8_114

Barratt Hacking, E., Cutter-Mackenzie, A., & Barratt, R. (2013). Children as active researchers. The potential of environmental education research involving children. In R. B. Stevenson, M. Brody, J. Dillon, & A. E. J. Wals (Eds.). *International handbook of research on environmental education* (pp. 438–458). Routledge.

Benjamin, T. E., Lucas-Thompson, R. G., Little, L. M., Davies, P. L., & Khetani, M. A. (2017). Participation in early childhood educational environments for young children with and without developmental disabilities and delays: A mixed methods study. *Physical & Occupational Therapy in Pediatircs, 37*(1), 87–107. https://doi.org/10.3109/01942638.2015.1130007

BERA. (2018). *Ethical guidelines for educational research* (4th ed.). British Educational Research Association (BERA). www.bera.ac.uk/publication/ethical-guidelines-for-educational-research-2018-online

Bergold, J., & Thomas, S. (2012). Participatory research methods: A methodological approach in motion. [110 paragraphs]. *Forum Qualitative Sozialforschung / Forum: Qualitative Social Research, 13*(1), Art. 30. http://nbn-resolving.de/urn:nbn:de:0114-fqs1201304

Bertam, T., Formosinho, J., Gray, C., Pascal, C., & Whalley, M. (2015). EECERA Ethical Code for Early Childhood Researchers. European Early Childhood Education Research Association (EECERA). www.eecera.org/wp-content/uploads/2016/07/EECERA-Ethical-Code.pdf

Bishop, K. (2014). Challenging research: Completing participatory social research with children and adolescents in a hospital setting. *HERD: Heard Environments Research & Design Journal, 7*(2), 76–91. https://doi.org/10.1177/193758671400700205

Blaisdell, C., McNair, L. J., Addison, L., & Davis, J. M. (2022). 'Why am I in all of these pictures?' From learning stories to lived stories: The politics of children's participation rights in documentation practices. *European Early Childhood Education Research Journal, 30*(4), 572–585. https://doi.org/10.1080/1350293X.2021.2007970

Bradbury-Jones, C., Isham, L., & Taylor, J. (2018). The complexities and contradictions in participatory research with vulnerable children and young people: A qualitative systematic review. *Social Science & Medicine, 215,* 80–91. https://doi.org/10.1016/j.socscimed.2018.08.038

Bryman, A., & Bell, E. (2019). *Social research methods* (5th ed.). Oxford University Press.

Cillessen, A. H. N., & Marks, P. E. L. (2017). Methodological choices in peer nomination research. *New Directions in Peer Nomination Methodology: New Directions for Child and Adolescent Development, 157,* 21–44. https://doi-org.ejournals.um.edu.mt/10.1002/cad.20206

Clark, A. (2005). Ways of seeing: Using the Mosaic approach to listen to young children's perspectives. In A. Clark, A. T. Kjørholt, & P. Moss (Eds.). *Beyond listening: Children's perspectives on early childhood services* (pp. 29–49). The Policy Press.

Clark, A. (2010). Young children as protagonists and the role of participatory, visual methods in engaging multiple perspectives. *American Journal of Community Psychology, 46*(1–2), 115–123. https://doi.org/10.1007/s10464-010-9332-y

Clark, A., & Moss, P. (2011). *Listening to young children: The Mosaic approach.* National Children's Bureau.

Clarke, V., Braun, V., Frith, H., & Moller, N. (2019). Editorial introduction to the special issue: Using story completion methods in qualitative research. *Qualitative Research in Psychology, 16*(1), 1–20. https://doi.org/10.1080/14780887.2018.1536378

Cohen, L., Manion, L., & Morrison, K. (2018). *Research methods in Education.* Routledge.

Corr, C., Snodgrass, M. R., Greene, J. C., Meadan, H., & Santos, R. M. (2020). Mixed methods in early childhood special education research: Purposes, challenges, and guidance. *Journal of Early Intervention, 42*(1), 20–30. https://doi.org/10.1177/1053815119873096

Coyne, I., Mallon, D., & Chubb, E. (2021). Researching with young children: Exploring the methodological advantages and challenges of using hand puppets and draw and tell. *Children & Society, 35*(5), 813–830. https://doi.org/10.1111/chso.12452

Creswell, J. W., & Plano Clark, V. L. (2018). *Designing and conducting mixed methods research* (3rd ed.). Sage.

Creswell, J. W., & Poth, C. N. (2018). *Qualitative inquiry and research design: Choosing among five approaches* (4th ed.). Sage.

Dahlberg, G., Moss, P., & Pence, A. (2013). *Beyond quality in early childhood education and care: Languages of evaluation.* Routledge.

Daly, A. (2020). Assessing children's capacity: Reconceptualising our understanding through the UN convention on the rights of the child. *The International Journal of Children's Rights, 28*(3), 471–499. https://doi.org/10.1163/15718182-02803011

Daly, A. (2022). Climate competence: Youth climate activism and its impact on international human rights law. *Human Rights Law Review, 22*(2), ngac011. https://doi.org/10.1093/hrlr/ngac011

Danby, S., & Farrell, A. (2004). Accounting for young children's competence in education research: New perspectives on research ethics. *Australian Educational Research, 31*(3), 35–50. https://doi.org/10.1007/BF03249527

Dawadi, S., Shrestha, S., & Giri, R. A. (2021). Mixed-methods research: A discussion on its types, challenges, and criticisms. *Journal of Practical Studies in Education, 2*(2), 25–36. https://doi.org/10.46809/jpse.v2i2.20

DeLay, D., Laursen, B., Kiuru, N., et al. (2021). A comparison of dyadic and social network assessments of peer influence. *International Journal of Behavioral Development, 45*(3), 275–288. https://doi.org/10.1177/0165025421992866

Dillman, D. A., Smyth, J. D., & Christian, L. M. (2014). *Internet, phone, mail and mixed-mode surveys: The tailored design method* (4th ed.). John Wiley & Sons.

Dockett, S., Einarsdottir, J., & Perry, B. (2009). Researching with children: Ethical tensions. *Journal of Early Childhood Research, 7*(3), 283–298. https://doi.org/10.1177/1476718X09336971

Dockett, S., Einarsdottir, J., & Perry, B. (2017). Photo elicitation: Reflecting on multiple sites of meaning. *International Journal of Early Years Education, 25* (3), 225–240. https://doi.org/10.1080/09669760.2017.1329713

Dockett, S., Main, S., & Kelly, L. (2011). Consulting young children: Experiences from a museum. *Visitor Studies, 14*(1), 13–33. https://doi.org/10.1080/10645578.2011.557626

Doyle, J., Edwards, D., & Haddow, A. (2022). Applying mixed methods research in large-scale programs: Tracing the long-term outcomes of development scholarship alumni. *Journal of Studies in International Education, 28*(1), 87–104. https://doi.org/10.1177/10283153221126246

Ebrahim, H., & Francis, D. (2008). You said, 'Black girl': Doing difference in early childhood. *Africa Education Review, 5*(2), 274–287. https://doi.org/10.1080/18146620802449894

Edwards, C., Gandini, L., & Forman, G. (2011). *The hundred languages of children: The Reggio Emilia experience in transformation*. Praeger.

Edwards, S. (2021). *Process quality, curriculum and pedagogy in early childhood education and care. OECD education working papers No. 247.*

OECD. www.oecd-ilibrary.org/docserver/eba0711e-en.pdf?expires=1670 225864&id=id&accname=guest&checksum=884B21A68603557818C458E BC3F4124A

Ellingson, L. L., & Sotirin, P. (2020). *Making data in qualitative research: Engagements, ethics, and entanglements.* Routledge.

Elwick, S. (2015). 'Baby-cam' and researching with infants: Viewer, image and (not)knowing. *Contemporary Issues in Early Childhood, 16*(4), 322–338. https://doi.org/10.1177/146394911561632

European Commission. (2021). *Early childhood education and care and the Covid-19 pandemic: Understanding and managing the impact of the crisis on the sector.* European Commission. https://data.europa.eu/doi/10.2766/60724

European Union. (2016). *Regulation (EU) 2016/679 of the European Parliament and the Council of 27 April 2016 on the protection of natural persons with regard to the processing of personal data and on the free movement of such data, and repealing Directive 95/46/EC (General Data Protection Regulation).* European Union. https://eur-lex.europa.eu/eli/reg/2016/679/oj

Fàbregues, S., Escalante-Barrios, E. L., Molina-Azorin, J. F., Hong, Q. N., & Verd, J. M. (2021). Taking a critical stance towards mixed methods research: A cross-disciplinary qualitative secondary analysis of researchers' views. *Plos One, 16*(7), e0252014. https://doi.org/10.1371/journal.pone.0252014

Fanghorban, R., Roudsari, R. L., & Taghipour, A. (2014). Skype interviewing: The new generation of online synchronous interview in qualitative research. *International Journal of Qualitative Studies on Health and Well-Being, 9,* 24152. http://dx.doi.org/10.3402/qhw.v9.24152

File, N., Mueller, J. J., Wisneski, D. B., & Stremmel, A. J. (2017). *Understanding research in early childhood education: Quantitative and qualitative methods.* Routledge.

Fleer, M., & van Oers, B. (Eds.). (2018). *International handbook of early childhood education, Vol. 1.* Springer Nature.

Fleet, A., & Harcourt, D. (2018). (Co)-researching with children. In M. Fleer, & B. van Oers (Eds.). *International handbook of early childhood education, Vol. 1* (pp. 165–201). Springer Nature.

Flewitt, R. S. (2022). Ethical provocations for early childhood research. In K. Kumpulainen, A. Kajamaa, O. Erstad, et al. (Eds.). *Nordic childhoods in the digital age: Insights into contemporary research on communication, learning and education* (pp. 207–213). Routledge.

Flewitt, R., & Ang, L. (2020). *Research methods for early childhood education.* Bloomsbury Academic.

Foucault, M. (1975). *Discipline and punish: The birth of the prison.* Random House.

Gallagher, M. (2009). Ethics. In E. K. M. Tisdall, J. Davis, & M. Gallegher (Eds.). *Researching with children and young people: Research design, methods and analysis* (pp. 11–28). Sage.

Gerholm, T., Kallioinen, P., Toner, S., et al. (2019). A randomized controlled trial to examine the effect of two teaching methods on preschool children's language and communication, executive functions, socioemotional comprehension, and early math skills. *BMC Psychology, 7*(59), 1–28. https://doi.org/10.1186/s40359-019-0325-9

Gilliat-Ray, S., Jacobs, S., Gregg, S. E., et al. (2022). Research ethics. In S. Engler, & M. Stausberg (Eds.). *The Routledge handbook of research methods in the study of religion* (pp. 88–109). Routledge.

Gold, Z. S., Perlman, J., Howe, N., et al. (2022). An observational study of children's problem solving during play with friends. *Journal of Cognition and Development, 24*(4), 503–523. https://doi.org/10.1080/15248372.2022.2058509

Gooding, P. (2021) The library in digital humanities: Interdisciplinary approaches to digital materials. In K. Schuster, & D. Stuart (Eds.). *Routledge international handbook of research methods in digital humanities* (pp. 137–152). Routledge Handbooks Online.

Gopalan, M., Rosinger, K., & Bin Ahn, J. (2020). Using quasi-experimental research design in education research: Growth, promise, and challenges. *Review of Research in Education, 44*, 218–243. https://doi.org/10.3102/0091732X20903302

Greig, A., Taylor, J., & MacKay, T. (2013). *Doing research with children: A practical guide.* Sage.

Guba, E. G., & Lincoln, Y. S. (2018). Competing paradigms in qualitative research. In N. K. Denzin, & Y. S. Lincoln (Eds.). *The Sage handbook of qualitative research* (pp. 173–202). Sage.

Guimond, F. A., Altman, R., Vitaro, F., Brendgen, M., & Laursen, B. (2022). The interchangeability of liking and friend nominations to measure peer acceptance and friendship. *International Journal of Behaviour Development, 46*(4), 358–367. https://doi.org/10.1177/01650254221084097

Hansen Sandseter, E. B., Stroli, R., & Sando, O. J. (2022). The dynamic relationship between outdoor environments and children's play. *Education 3–13, 50*(1), 97–110. https://doi.org/10.1080/03004279.2020.1833063

Harrison, L. J., & Wang, C. (2018). Current approaches in quantitative research in early childhood education. In M. Fleer, & B. van Oers (Eds.). *International handbook of early childhood education, Vol. 1* (pp. 295–316). Springer Nature.

Hart, R. A. (1992). *Children's participation: From tokenism to citizenship.* UNICEF. www.unicef-irc.org/publications/pdf/childrens_participation.pdf

Hirosawa, E., & Oga-Baldwin, W. L. O. (2023). Surveys and questionnaires with young language learners. In Y. G. Butler, & B. H. Haung (Eds.). *Research methods for understanding child second language development.* Routledge.

Hoyte, F., Degotardi, S., & Torr, J. (2015). What it is all about: Topic choices in young children's play. *International Journal of Play, 4*(2), 136–148. http://dx.doi.org/10.1080/21594937.2015.1060566

James, A., Jenks, C., & Prout, A. (1998). *Theorizing childhood.* Polity Press.

James, A., & Prout, A. (2015). *Constructing and reconstructing childhood: Contemporary issues in the sociological study of childhood.* Routledge.

Johnson, V., Colwell, J., & Hart, R. (2014). *Steps to engaging young children in research. Volume 2: The researcher toolkit.* Education Research Centre, University of Brighton. https://doi.org/10.13140/RG.2.2.22139.82720

Kähler, J., Hahn, I., & Köller, O. (2020). The development of early scientific literacy gaps in kindergarten children. *International Journal of Science Education, 42*(12), 1988–2007. https://doi.org/10.1080/09500693.2020.1808908

Koller, D., & Murphy, E. (2022). Dolls as a rights-affirming early childhood research method. *The International Journal of Children's Rights, 30*(4), 922–956. https://doi.org/10.1163/15718182-30040005

Lahman, M. K. E. (2018). *Ethics in social science research: Becoming culturally responsive.* Sage.

Laursen, B. (2015). I don't quite get it … Personal experiences within the person-oriented approach. *Journal of Person-Oriented Research, 1*(1-2), 42-47. https://doi.org/10.17505/jpor.2015.05

Laursen, B., Legget-James, M. P., & Valdes, O. M. (2023). Relative likeability and relative popularity as sources of influence in children's friendships. *PLoS ONE, 18*(5), e0283117. https://doi.org/10.1371/journal.pone.0283117

Lazar, I., Darlington, R., Murray, H., et al. (1982). Lasting effects of early education: A report from the consortium for longitudinal studies. *Monographs of the Society for Research in Child Development, 47*(2/3), i, iii, v–vii, ix–xiv, 1–151. https://doi.org/10.2307/1165938

LeMasters, A. C., & Vandermaas-Peeler, M. (2023). Exploring outdoor play: A mixed-methods study of the quality of preschool play environments and teacher perceptions of risky play. *Journal of Adventure Education and Outdoor, 23*(1), 1–13. https://doi.org/10.1080/14729679.2021.1925564

Lenette, C., Vaughan, P., & Boydell, K. (2022). How can story completion be used in culturally safe ways? *International Journal of Qualitative Methods, 21*(ahead of print). https://doi.org/10.1177/16094069221077764

Liebenberg, L., & Ungar, U. (2015). Using mixed methods in research with young children across cultures and contexts. In O. N. Saracho (Ed.). *Handbook of research methods in early childhood education: Review of research methodologies, Vol. 1* (pp. 383–402). Information Age.

Loebach, J., & Cox, A. (2022). Playing in 'the backyard': Environmental features and conditions of a natural playspace which support diverse outdoor play activities among younger children. *International Journal of Environmental Research and Public Health, 19*(10), 12661. https://doi.org/ 10.3390/ijerph191912661

Luken, M. M., & Sauzet, O. (2021). Patterning strategies in early childhood: A mixed methods study examining 3- to 5-year-old children's patterning competencies. *Mathematical Thinking and Learning, 23*(1), 28–48. https:// doi.org/10.1080/10986065.2020.1719452

Lundy, L. (2007). 'Voice' is not enough: Conceptualising article 12 of the United Nations convention on the rights of the child. *British Educational Research Journal, 33*(6), 927–942. https://doi.org/10.1080/0141192070 1657033

MacDonald, C. (2009). The importance of identity and policy: The case for and of children. *Children and Society, 23*(4), 241–251. https://doi.org/10.1111/ j.1099-0860.2008.00170.x

MacNaughton, G. (2005). *Doing Foucault in early childhood studies*. Routledge.

MacNaughton, G., Hughes, P., & Smith, K. (2008). *Young children as active citizens: Principles, policies and pedagogies*. Cambridge Scholars.

Marks, P. E. L. (2017). Introduction to the special issue: 20th-Century origins and 21st-Century developments of peer nomination methodology. *New Directions in Peer Nomination Methodology: New Directions for Child and Adolescent Development, 157*, 7–19. https://doi-org.ejournals.um.edu.mt/ 10.1002/cad.20205

Mason, J. (2018). *Qualitative researching* (3rd ed.). Sage.

Mehari, K. R., Waasdrop, T. E., & Leff, S. S. (2019). Measuring relational and overt aggression by peer report: A comparison of peer nominations and peer ratings. *Journal of School Violence, 18*(3), 362–374. https://doi-org.ejour nals.um.edu.mt/10.1080/15388220.2018.1504684

Melhuish, E., Belsky, J., Leyland, A. H., Barnes, J., & The National Evaluation of Sure Start Research Team. (2008). Effects of fully-established Sure Start Local Programmes on 3-year-old children and their families living in England: A quasi-experimental observational study. *The Lancet, 372*, 1641–1647. https://doi.org/10.1016/S0140-6736(08)61667-0

Mertens, D. M. (2009). *Transformative research and evaluation*. Guilford Press.

Mertens, D. M. (2015). *Evaluation in education and psychology: Integrating diversity with quantitative, qualitative, and mixed methods*. Sage.

Messinger, D. S., Prince, E. B., Zheng, M., et al. (2019). Continuous measurement of dynamic classroom social interactions. *International Journal of Behavioral Development, 43*(3), 263–270. https://doi.org/10.1177/01650254 18820708

Miller, V. A., & Nelson, R. M. (2006). A developmental approach to child assent for nontherapeutic research. *The Journal of Pediatrics, 149*(1), s25–s30. https://doi.org/10.1016/j.jpeds.2006.04.047

Moller, N. P., Clarke, V., Braun, V., Tischner, I., & Vossler, A. (2021). Qualitative story completion for counseling psychology research: A creative method to interrogate dominant discourses. *Journal of Counseling Psychology, 68*(3), 286–298. https://doi.org/10.1037/cou0000538

Morrow, V. (2008). Dilemmas in children's participation in England. In A. Invernizzi, & J. Williams (Eds.). *Children and citizenship* (pp. 120–130). Sage.

Mukherji, P., & Albon, D. (2018). *Research methods in early childhood: An introductory guide*. Sage.

Nguyen, K. T. N. H., Stuart, J. J., Shah, A. H., et al. (2023). Novel methods for leveraging large cohort studies for qualitative and mixed methods research. *American Journal of Epidemiology, 192*(5), 821–829. https://doi.org/ 10.1093/aje/kwad030

Nur, I., & Arnas, Y. A. (2022). Turkish preschool children's representations of friendship: Story completion method adaptation study. *International Journal of Assessment Tools in Education, 9*(2), 357–375. https://doi.org/10.21449/ ijate.958145

OECD. (2018). *Engaging young children: Lessons from research about quality in early childhood education and care, starting strong*. OECD. https://doi .org/10.1787/9789264085145-en

OECD. (2022a). *Early childhood education and care workforce development: A foundation process quality*. OECD. www.oecd-ilibrary.org/docserver/ e012efc0-en.pdf?expires=1670225921&id=id&accname=guest&checksum= 9B6F69E3A5FD5064F94FEEE4D3491FC9

OECD. (2022b). *Education at a glance 2022: OECD indicators*. OECD. www .oecd-ilibrary.org/education/education-at-a-glance-2022_3197152b-en

O'Farrelly, C., & Tatlow-Golden, M. (2022). It is up to you if you want to take part. Supporting young children's informed choice about research participation with simple visual booklets. *European Early Childhood Education Research Journal, 30*(1), 63–80. https://doi.org/10.1080/1350293X.2022 .2026434

Pearce, L. (2012). Mixed methods inquiry in sociology. *American Behavioral Scientist, 56*(6), 829–848. https://doi.org/10.1177/000276421 1433798

Perry, L. K., Mitsven, S. G., Custode, S., et al. (2022). Reciprocal patterns of peer speech in preschoolers with and without hearing loss. *Early Childhood Quarterly, 60,* 201–213. https://doi.org/10.1016/j.ecresq.2022.02.003

Piaget, J. (1952). *The origins of intelligence in children.* International Universities Press.

Plano Clark, V. L., & Ivankova, N. V. (2016). *Mixed methods research: A guide to the field.* Sage.

Plucker, J. A., & Makel, M. C. (2021). Replication is important for educational psychology: Recent developments and key issues. *Educational Psychologist, 56*(2), 90–100. https://doi.org/10.1080/00461520.2021.1895796

Prout, A. (2005). *The future of childhood: Towards the interdisciplinary study of children.* Routledge Falmer.

Prout, A. (2011). Taking a step away from modernity: Reconsidering the new sociology of childhood. *Global Studies Childhood, 1*(1), 4–14. https://doi .org/10.2304/gsch.2011.1.1.4

Prout, A., & James, A. (1997). A new paradigm for the sociology of childhood? In A. James, & A. Prout (Eds.). *Constructing and reconstructing childhood: Contemporary issues in the sociological study of childhood* (2nd ed., pp. 7–33). Routledge.

Punch, S. (2002). Research with children: The same or different from research with adults? *Childhood, 9*(3), 321–341. https://doi.org/10.1177/0907568202 009003005

Qvortrup, J. (2006). Editorial: Are children subjects or a liability? *Childhood, 13*(4), 435–439. https://doi.org/10.1177/0907568206068555

Rinaldi, C. (2021). *In dialogue with Reggio Emilia: Listening, researching and learning* (2nd ed.). Routledge.

Rogoff, B. (2003). *The cultural nature of human development.* Oxford University Press.

Roni, S. M., Merga, M. K., & Morris, J. E. (2020). *Conducting quantitative research in education.* Springer Nature Singapore.

Roth-Cline, M., & Nelson, R. M. (2013). Parental permission and child assent in research on children. *Yale Journal of Biology and Medicine, 86*(3), 291–301. PMID: 24058304, PMCID: PMC3767214

Sammons, P., Siraj-Blatchford, I., Sylva, K., et al. (2005). Investigating the effect of pre-school provision: Using mixed methods in the EPPE research. *International Journal of Social Research and Methodology, 8*(5), 207–224. https://doi.org/10.1080/13645570500154840

Schwartzman, H. B. (1976). The anthropological study of children's play. *Annual Review of Anthropology, 5*, 289–328. https://doi.org/10.1146/annurev.an.05.100176.001445

Scott, D., & Usher, R. (2011). *Researching education: Data methods and theory in educational enquiry*. Bloomsbury.

Sheridan, M. D. (2008). *From birth to five years: Children's developmental progress*. Routledge.

Shier, H. (2001). Pathways to participation: Openings, opportunities and obligations. *Children and Society, 15*, 107–17. https://doi.org/10.1002/chi.617

Siagian, C., Habib, M., Bennouna, C., et al. (2021). *Handbook for children's participation in research in Indonesia*. PUSKAPA.

Sivertsen, A. H., & Moe, B. (2022). Four-to-six-year-old children's experiences of participating in different physical environments and activities in early childhood education and care institutions in Norway. *Education 3–13, 50*(7), 857–867. https://doi.org/10.1080/03004279.2021.1914703

Slot, P. (2018). *Structural characteristics and processes of quality early childhood education and care: A literature review. OECD working papers No. 176*. OECD. www.oecd-ilibrary.org/docserver/edaf3793-en.pdf?expires=1670225846&id=id&accname=guest&checksum=923119C26ADA60D23A691BEDE1158BC7

Spiteri, J. (2016). *Young children's perceptions of environmental sustainability: A Maltese perspective*. Unpublished PhD thesis. Edinburgh: The University of Edinburgh.

Spiteri, J. (2020). A reflection on research methods that engage young children with environmental sustainability. *An Leanbh Og, 13*(1), 149–170. https://omepireland.ie/wp-content/uploads/2020/08/AN-LEANBH-OG-VOL13.pdf

Stake, R. E. (2006). *Multiple case study analysis*. The Guildford Press.

Stenger, K. M., Ritter-Gooder, P. K., Perry, C., & Albercht, J. A. (2014). A mixed methods study of food safety knowledge, practices and beliefs in Hispanic families with young children. *Appetite, 83*, 194–201. https://doi.org/10.1016/j.appet.2014.08.034

Stephenson, A. (2009). Horses in the sandpit: Photography, prolonged involvement and 'stepping back' as strategies for listening to children's voices. *Early Child Development and Care, 179*(2), 13–41. https://doi.org/10.1080/03004430802667047

Stroli, R., & Hansen Sandseter, E. B. (2019). Children's play, well-being and involvement: How children play indoors and outdoors in Norwegian early childhood education and care institutions. *International Journal of Play, 8*(1), 65–78. https://doi.org/10.1080/21594937.2019.1580338

Sun, Y., Blewitt, C., Edwards, S., et al. (2023). Methods and ethics in qualitative research exploring young children's voice: A systematic review. *International Journal of Qualitative Methods, 22*(ahead of print). https://doi.org/10.1177/16094069231152449

Syrjämäkia, M., Reunamob, J., Pesonenc, H., Pirttimaad, R., & Kontu, E. (2023). The involvement of autistic children in early childhood education. *European Journal of Special Needs Education* (ahead of print), 1–15. https://doi.org/10.1080/08856257.2023.2179310

Tashakkori, A., & Creswell, J. W. (2007). Editorial: The new era of mixed methods. *Journal of Mixed Methods Research, 1*, 3–7. https://doi.org/10.1177/2345678906293042

Teddlie, C., & Tashakkori, A. (2009). *Foundations of mixed methods research.* Sage.

Templeton, M., Cuevas-Parra, P., & Lundy, L. (2023). Children's participation in international fora: The experience and perspectives of children and adults. *Children & Society, 37*, 786–805. https://doi.org/10.1111/chso.12629

Thorpe, L. P. (1946). *Child psychology and development.* The Ronald Press.

Thunberg, S., & Arnell, L. (2022). Pioneering the use of technologies in qualitative research – A research review of the use of digital interviews. *International Journal of Social Research Methodology, 25*(6), 757–768. https://doi.org/10.1080/13645579.2021.1935565

Tisdall, E. K. M. (2010). Not so 'new'? Looking critically at childhood studies. *Exploring children's relationships across minority and majority worlds.* ESRC Seminar Series, 29 April 2010. www.academia.edu/1970598/Not_So_New_Looking_Critically_at_Childhood_Studies

Tisdall, E. K. M. (2015). Children and young people's participation: A critical consideration of Article 12. In W. Vandenhole, E. Desmet, D. Reynaert, & S. Lembrechts (Eds.). *Routledge international handbook of children's rights studies* (pp. 185–200). Routledge.

Tisdall, E. K. M., & Cuevas-Parra, P. (2022). Beyond the familiar challenges for children and young people's participation rights: The potential of activism. *The International Journal of Human Rights, 26*(5), 792–810. https://doi.org/10.1080/13642987.2021.1968377

Tisdall, E. K. M. & Punch, S. (2012). Not so new? Looking critically at childhood studies. *Children's Geographies, 10*(3), 249–264. https://doi.org/10.1080/14733285.2012.693376

UN Committee on the Rights of the Child. (2009). *General comment No. 12 (2009): The right of the child to be heard.* Office of the UN High Commissioner for Human Rights. www2.ohchr.org/english/bodies/crc/docs/advanceversions/crc-c-gc-12.pdf

UNESCO. (2017). *Early childhood care and education*. UNESCO. http://en
.unesco.org/themes/early-childhood-care-and-education

UNESCO. (2020). *Education for sustainable development: A roadmap*.
UNESCO. www.gcedclearinghouse.org/sites/default/files/resources/
200782eng.pdf

UNESCO. (2023). *What you need to know about early childhood care and
education*. UNESCO Digital Library. www.unesco.org/en/early-childhood-
education/need-know

UNICEF. (2019). *An environment fit for children: UNICEF's approach to climate
change*. UNICEF. www.unicef.org/media/73331/file/An-Environment-
Fit-for-Children-2019.pdf

United Nations. (1989). *United Nations convention on the rights of the child*.
Office of the UN High Commissioner for Human Rights. www.ohchr.org/en/
instruments-mechanisms/instruments/convention-rights-child

United Nations. (2015). *Transforming our world. The 2030 agenda for sustainable development A/RES/70/1*. United Nations Department of Economic and
Social Affairs Sustainable Development. https://sdgs.un.org/2030agenda

Urbina-Garcia, A., Jindal-Snape, D., Lindsay, A., et al. (2021). Voices of young
children aged 3–7 years in educational research: An international systematic
literature review. *European Early Childhood Education Research Journal*,
30(1), 8–31. http://doi.org/10.1080/1350293X.2021.1992466

Vaughn, L. M., & Jacquez, F. (2020). Participatory research methods – Choice
points in the research process. *Journal of Participatory Research Methods*,
1(1). https://doi.org/10.35844/001c.13244

Vygotsky, L. S. (1971). *The psychology of art*. MIT Press.

Vygotsky, L. S. (1978). *Mind in society: Development of higher psychological
processes*. Harvard University Press.

White, H., & Sabarwal, S. (2014). *Quasi-experimental design and methods*.
Methodological Briefs, Impact Evaluation No. 8. UNICEF. www.unicef-irc
.org/KM/IE/img/downloads/Quasi-Experimental_Design_and_Methods_ENG
.pdf

WMA Declaration of Helsinki. (6 September 2022). *WMA declaration of
Helsinki: Ethical principles for medical research involving human subjects*.
Ferney-Voltaire WMA The World Medical Association. www.wma.net/pol
icies-post/wma-declaration-of-helsinki-ethical-principles-for-medical-
research-involving-human-subjects/

Wu, C., Zhang, Q., Liu, S., Wang, L., & Zhao, Q. (2022). Child executive
function linking marital adjustment to peer nominations of prosocial
behaviour. *Journal of Marriage and Family, 85*, 829–844. https://doi.org/
10.1111/jomf.12892

Yamaguchi, S., Bentayeb, N., Holtom, A., et al. (2022). Participation of children and youth in mental health policymaking: A scoping review (Part 1). *Administration and Policy in Mental Health and Mental Health Services Research*, 50, 58–83. https://doi.org/10.1007/s10488-022-01223-0

Cambridge Elements ≡

Research Methods for Developmental Science

Brett Laursen
Florida Atlantic University

Brett Laursen is a Professor of Psychology at Florida Atlantic University. He is Editor-in-Chief of the *International Journal of Behavioral Development*, where he previously served as the founding Editor of the Methods and Measures section. Professor Laursen received his Ph.D. in Child Psychology from the Institute of Child Development at the University of Minnesota and an Honorary Doctorate from Örebro University, Sweden. He is a Docent Professor of Educational Psychology at the University of Helsinki, and a Fellow of the American Psychological Association (Division 7, Developmental), the Association for Psychological Science, and the International Society for the Study of Behavioural Development. Professor Laursen is the co-editor of the *Handbook of Developmental Research Methods* and the *Handbook of Peer Interactions, Relationships, and Groups*.

About the Series

Each offering in this series will focus on methodological innovations and contemporary strategies to assess adjustment and measure change, empowering scholars of developmental science who seek to optimally match their research questions to pioneering methods and quantitative analyses.

Research Methods for Developmental Science

Printed in the United States
by Baker & Taylor Publisher Services